Best wishes!
I hope you enjoyed LMT 2017 event.

Economic Impact or Contribution

Best regards
[signature]

Economic Impact or Contribution

Essays on Business and Community Relations

Murat Arik

LEXINGTON BOOKS
Lanham • Boulder • New York • London

Published by Lexington Books
An imprint of The Rowman & Littlefield Publishing Group, Inc.
4501 Forbes Boulevard, Suite 200, Lanham, Maryland 20706
www.rowman.com

Unit A, Whitacre Mews, 26-34 Stannary Street, London SE11 4AB

Copyright © 2015 by Lexington Books

All rights reserved. No part of this book may be reproduced in any form or by any electronic or mechanical means, including information storage and retrieval systems, without written permission from the publisher, except by a reviewer who may quote passages in a review.

British Library Cataloguing in Publication Information Available

Library of Congress Control Number: 2015955991
ISBN: 978-1-4985-1695-2 (cloth : alk. paper)
eISBN: 978-1-4985-1696-9

∞™ The paper used in this publication meets the minimum requirements of American National Standard for Information Sciences—Permanence of Paper for Printed Library Materials, ANSI/NISO Z39.48-1992.

Printed in the United States of America

For Hulya Arik,

My Parents, Omer and Fadima, and

My Students at Business and Economic Research Center

Contents

Preface		xiii
1	Introduction and Overview	1
	The Plan of the Book	2
2	Assumptions, Methods, and Concepts	5
	Contributions versus Impact	6
	Assumptions and Definitions	6
	Cost-Benefit Analysis	7
	Counterfactual Analysis	7
	Survey Data versus Secondary Data Analysis	8
	Input-Output Models	8
	Regional Context	9
3	Health Care Industry Cluster and Regional Economy	11
	Introduction	11
	Overview of the Core Health Care Industry	12
	National Trends	13
	Trends in Tennessee	14
	Trends in the Nashville MSA	15
	Comparative Perspective on Trends in the Core Health Care Industry	16
	Study Goals and Methodology	16
	Goals of the Study	16
	A Review of Selected Literature	17
	Method and Data	18
	Definitions	19
	Conceptual Framework for Impact Analysis	19

Core Health Care Industry in Nashville: Its Scope and Trend	20
Total Employment	20
Sectoral Diversity	21
Establishments	22
Wages	22
Export Potential of Core Health Care Industry Segments	23
Relative Growth Performance of Core Health Care Segments	23
Core Health Care Industry and the Local Economy	24
Nashville's Health Care Industry Cluster	24
Employment and Office Space	25
Establishments and Wages	26
Investor-Owned Health Care Management Companies (Public and Private)	26
Economic Impact of the Nashville Health Care Cluster	28
Employment Impact	28
Business Revenue Impact	29
Personal Income	29
Fiscal Impact of the Nashville Health Care Industry Cluster	30
Nashville's Core Health Care Industry from a Comparative Perspective	30
Export Potential and Employment Growth	30
Health Care Industry Cluster Headquarters and Global Impact	31
Health Care Occupations	31
Venture Capital Flow	31
Where Does the Nashville MSA Stand Relative to Its Peers?	32
Nashville Health Care Council (NHCC) Member Companies	34
Survey Methodology	34
NHCC Member Companies—Employment and Wages	35
NHCC Members: Office Space and Revenues	36
NHCC Members: CEO Confidence Survey	37
Notes	39
4 Higher Education Institutions in Middle Tennessee: An In-Depth Analysis of Their Impact on the Region from a Comparative Perspective	43
Economic Growth, Knowledge, and Universities: An Introduction	43
Overview	43
Economic Growth	44
Knowledge	45
Universities	45
Economic Impact of Universities	46

Study Goals	48
General Methodology	48
Economic Impact of Higher Education Institutions in Middle Tennessee: Input-Output Analysis	50
Overview	50
An Overview of Economic Impact Studies	50
Study Assumptions	51
Methodology	52
Economic Impact Categories, Assumptions, and Impact Results	54
Total Higher Education Economic Impact	59
Conclusion	61
Higher Education Institutions and Skilled Labor Supply and Demand in Middle Tennessee	61
Overview	61
Methodology	63
Profile of Enrollment and Graduates: Supply Side	64
Demand for Workforce and Educational Characteristics of Occupations	66
Business Community—Higher Education Institutions in Middle Tennessee	68
Overview	68
Methodology	69
Higher Education Institutions in the Business Community	70
Survey Findings	71
Conclusion and Discussions	72
Higher Education Institutions in Middle Tennessee from a Comparative Perspective	74
Overview	74
Methodology	75
A Profile of Middle Tennessee	76
Indicators of Higher Education	77
Conclusion and Discussions	83
Notes	84
5 The Nonprofit Sector in the Nashville MSA	87
Introduction	87
Literature Review and Methodology	88
Literature Review	88
Geography and Scope of the Nonprofit Sector	88
Economic Impact Definition and IMPLAN Software	89
Data and Data Sources	91

Characteristics of the Nonprofit Sector and the Nashville MSA Economy	92
Size, Scope and Change by Segment	92
The Nonprofit Sector and the Nashville MSA Economy	97
Economic Assessment of the Nonprofit Sector	97
Economic Impact—Export Component	98
Economic Impact by Segment	99
Economic Impact by Major Industries	100
Economic Contributions—Total Spending	101
Economic Contributions by Segment	101
Economic Contribution by Major Industry	102
Economic Contributions plus Volunteering	103
Recession Crisis Management and Nonprofits in the Nashville MSA	104
A Comparative Perspective on the Nonprofit Sector in the Nashville MSA	105

6 The Northwest Tennessee Regional Port of Cates Landing:

An Economic Analysis	111
Introduction	111
Study Area	111
Project Background: NWTRP at Cates Landing	112
History	112
Proposed Investment	113
Study Goals and Research Questions	114
Study Region at a Glance: Indicators of Socioeconomic Distress	114
Study Region's General Characteristics	115
Employment and Unemployment	115
Population Growth	115
Income	116
Poverty	116
Conceptual Framework, Assumptions, and Data	117
Cargo Volume and Long-Term Job Creation	118
Public Benefits and Local Impact	120
Assumptions and Data	120
Findings	122
Long-Term Outcomes	124
Evaluation of Cost-Benefit Indicators	127
Job Creation and Economic Stimulus	128
Port Construction	129
Implications of Proposed Investment for the Regional Economy: Indicators of Distress Revisited	130
Wage	130

	Unemployment	131
	Poverty	131
7	Economic Impact of Bonnaroo Music Festival on Coffee County	137
	A Profile of Coffee County and Bonnaroo	137
	Study Assumptions and Method	138
	A General Visitor Profile	140
	Conceptual Framework for Economic Impact Analysis	142
	Economic and Fiscal Impact of Bonnaroo Music Festival	142
	Economic Impact	142
	Fiscal Impact	144
	Secondary Data Analysis	144
	Chronological Clustering Analysis	145
	Hierarchical Clustering Analysis	146
	Regime Shift Analysis	147
	Conclusion	148
8	Recommendations from the Field	149
Bibliography		151
Index		161
About the Author		165

Preface

Why do we need to conduct an economic and fiscal assessment? How can we create one? Once it is created, how can we use the completed study to make a difference in the region? These are critical questions I've been asked repeatedly over the past 16 years by different organizations, associations, businesses, and community leaders. In fact, most often when community leaders approach me, their concerns are related to these three questions, but the scope of the issue is not fully clear. In most cases, it is the job of applied regional economists, management strategists, or professional consultants to help formulate the first question, answer the second, and provide direction in response to the third. Whatever business and economic issue one is dealing with, the answers to these questions should be based on a solid methodological framework in order to maintain the integrity of the scientific research process.

Economic Impact or Contribution contributes to the applied regional economic literature by (1) providing a framework for handling a diverse set of projects and (2) providing detailed case studies of actual fieldwork regarding the health care industry, higher education institutions, the nonprofit sector, infrastructure investment, and a major musical entertainment event. *Economic Impact or Contribution* accomplishes three major tasks by answering the following questions: (1) What are the differences between the economic concepts used in economic versus fiscal assessment studies? (2) How can we structure an economic and business issue or challenge? (3) How can we create a research product that helps the project's sponsors solve their problem?

Over the past 12 years, I've been honored to serve communities across Tennessee in various capacities as part of the Business and Economic Research Center (BERC) in Jones College of Business at Middle Tennessee State University. *Economic Impact or Contribution* introduces some of the major research projects I've been involved in at BERC to both academic and professional communities. Of course, none of these research projects could have come to fruition without the generous support of community leaders, business associations, and businesses themselves. *Economic Impact or Contribution* includes several studies that required more than a year to complete. In the process, several graduate and undergraduate students have received financial support for their education and grown professionally.

All five case studies introduced in *Economic Impact or Contribution* were sponsored by businesses, community organizations, or business associations. Chapter 3, for example, introduces a comprehensive assessment of the health care industry cluster in the Nashville MSA in 2010. This study was sponsored by Nashville Health Care Council (NHCC). The study in chapter 4 on higher education institutions in Middle Tennessee took more than a year to complete. This first-ever attempt to quantify the contributions of 20 major universities to the Middle Tennessee economy was sponsored by Belmont and Vanderbilt universities under the leadership of the Greater Nashville Area Chamber of Commerce.

Sponsored by the Center for Nonprofit Management, chapter 5 analyzes the size and scope of the nonprofit sector in the Nashville MSA. Chapter 6 differs slightly from the other chapters in that it deals with the cost-benefit assessment of infrastructure investment in the Port at Cates Landing in Northwest Tennessee. This study was sponsored by the Northwest Tennessee Regional Port Authority. Finally, the study in chapter 7 analyzes the economic and fiscal impact of Bonnaroo Music Festival, sponsored by the event's organizer, Axis Venture LLC.

In preparing *Economic Impact or Contribution*, I benefited from the intellectual contributions of many graduate and undergraduate students and staff members. I thank all of them for their invaluable contributions. However, I must mention two individuals who spent endless hours bringing the pieces together to make this book happen: BERC senior editor Sally Govan for editorial support and BERC undergraduate research associate Allison Logan for reviewing and rewriting the manuscript chapters. Furthermore, my special thanks go to the presidents of 20 universities in Middle Tennessee for rallying in support of a comprehensive study of higher education institutions in the region.

Finally, any endeavor of this magnitude requires sacrifices: I would like to dedicate this book to my wife, Hulya, and two sons, Berat and Batu, for supporting me in pursuing my professional goals.

Murat Arik
Middle Tennessee State University
Murfreesboro, TN
August 31, 2015

Chapter 1

Introduction and Overview

What do we mean when we talk about *economic impact*? How is *economic impact* different from *economic contribution*? What are the underlying assumptions of an economic and fiscal assessment of an industry cluster? What are the major steps in conducting a cost-benefit analysis of a public infrastructure investment? What role do higher education institutions play in their communities? As students of applied regional economics or strategic management, we often face these or similar questions in our professional life. Each time we are asked such questions, we naturally comb through the existing literature for materials relevant to framing the questions and laying the groundwork for a research initiative.

Economic Impact or Contribution has emerged as an answer to many research-related questions in dealing with regional business and economic issues and challenges. *Economic Impact or Contribution* is not a theoretical analysis of regional economic issues; rather, it presents a roadmap to help applied regional economists, economic development professionals, and students of strategic management address regional economic issues or challenges and inform sound public policy direction.

Economic Impact or Contribution starts with a basic question: What are the underlying assumptions and concepts used in economic and fiscal assessments? This question is answered by defining the following major—sometimes controversial—concepts: (1) economic impact or contribution; (2) cost-benefit analysis; (3) counterfactual approach; (4) survey data or secondary data; (5) input-output models; and (6) regional context. Many of these concepts and associated assumptions are critically important in conducting economic and fiscal assessments of events, industries, investments, or organizations as they help us frame the research questions and systematically address them. In addition to providing definitions and explanations, in order to help the reader better understand these concepts, *Economic Impact or Contribution* features five carefully selected major studies on diverse topics ranging from the health care industry to a music festival.

THE PLAN OF THE BOOK

Economic Impact or Contribution is divided into eight chapters. Chapter 2 introduces and explains underlying assumptions and concepts widely used in economic and fiscal assessment studies. Chapter 3 introduces a comprehensive analysis of the health care industry cluster in the Nashville MSA. As a major economic driver in both the region and the nation, the health care industry figures prominently in the agenda of both economic development professionals and community leaders. This chapter broadly discusses the health care industry cluster by answering the following six questions: (1) What are the trends, scope, and impact of the core health care industry and health care industry cluster in the regional economy? (2) What is the economic significance to the region of health care companies headquartered in Nashville? (3) How does Nashville's health care industry compare with the health care industry in 12 of its peer MSAs? (4) How does the Nashville MSA rank relative to its 12 peer MSAs in terms of selected health care indicators? (5) What is the economic significance of Nashville Health Care Council (NHCC) members to the regional economy? (6) What are the expectations of NHCC member company CEOs for the national and local economies?

Chapter 4 starts with the following broad research question: What role do higher education institutions play in the region's economy? In other words, what does it mean for a region to host 100,000 students annually? The implications of the presence of 100,000 students in 20 higher education institutions were analyzed under the following major categories: (1) the knowledge economy and higher education institutions, (2) labor supply and demand, (3) economic and fiscal impact assessments, (4) interaction between the business community and higher education, and (5) a comparative perspective on higher education institutions in Middle Tennessee.

Chapter 5 presents a recent case study on the role of the nonprofit sector in the Nashville MSA economy. Similar to the analyses in chapters 3 and 4, the analysis of the nonprofit sector is comprehensive. It answers the following four questions: (1) What is the scope and size of the Nashville MSA's nonprofit sector? (2) How has the Nashville MSA's nonprofit sector evolved over the years? (3) How has the Nashville MSA's nonprofit sector managed the economic downturn? (4) How does the Nashville MSA's nonprofit sector compare with that of peer MSAs?

How does one conduct a cost-benefit analysis of a public infrastructure project? Chapter 6 answers this question by demonstrating step by step an assessment of the return on investment for a port investment in northwest Tennessee. The goals of this chapter were (1) to provide a brief assessment of socioeconomic conditions in the three-county region (Dyer, Lake, and Obion) from a comparative perspective; (2) to provide an assessment of public benefits of the proposed investment in Cates Landing; (3) to describe and analyze the short-term economic impact of construction spending related to the proposed infrastructure, including but not limited to basic and enhanced site development and infrastructure, terminal dock site development and infrastructure, harbor and navigation lighting, and energy efficient (green) technology; (4) to describe and analyze the long-term economic impact of the proposed development of the Port of Cates Landing on the region's economy; and (5) to provide a brief assessment of the implications of the port investment for socioeconomic dynamics in the region. In line with these five goals, this chapter seeks answers to the following major questions: (1) What are the indicators of economic distress, and how is the study region faring compared to the U.S.? (2) Do public benefits from the port justify the $20-million investment? (3) What are the regional impacts of the Port of Cates Landing? (4) What are the implications of the Port of Cates Landing for the indicators of socioeconomic distress?

What impact does a camp-based music festival have on a rural county's economy? Chapter 7 looks at the economic and fiscal impact of the Bonnaroo Music and Arts Festival on Coffee County, Tennessee. This chapter uses a variety of research tools to measure the festival's impact after five consecutive successful years (as of 2007). In conclusion, chapter 8 offers major takeaways from the case studies for students of applied regional economy and strategic management.

Chapter 2

Assumptions, Methods, and Concepts

A regional economic and fiscal assessment should be based on carefully established assumptions and conceptual frameworks. What are some of the concepts widely (*mis*)used in economic and fiscal assessment literature? Chapter 2 provides a brief review of major concepts and methods used by both applied economists and business consultants in conducting economic and fiscal assessments. Some of the constructs used in estimating the economic and fiscal impact of a business, industry, or event are often misunderstood. In addition to chapter 2, the case study chapters provide additional details on the wide range of concepts involved in economic impact assessment.

What are some major controversial concepts in economic assessments? What underlying assumptions should professionals pay close attention to when dealing with certain constructs in calculating multiplier effects? What are some methods and tools used to calculate economic and fiscal assessments? This chapter's first area of focus is whether one is measuring economic impact or contribution when assessing the role of an event or industry in a community.

The second concept we address is how cost-benefit analysis (CBA) differs from economic impact assessment. What is required to calculate a CBA? What critical assumptions should one make when conducting a CBA of a public investment? The third issue this chapter investigates is the concept of counterfactual analysis. Often the industry or organization whose contribution to a local economy we are assessing has already been a part of the economic structure. How can we deal with such a situation? In this context, we briefly introduce the concept of counterfactual analysis.

The fourth issue is the nature of data used in assessing the role of an organization or industry. Data availability is a big concern for many researchers, and collecting primary data is often cost prohibitive. The fifth issue is related to the methods used in calculating economic and fiscal contributions. Several input-output models have been widely used. Finally, as the regional context is critical, researchers must choose an appropriate regional boundary for calculating the indirect and induced effect of direct spending or employment in a region.

CONTRIBUTIONS VERSUS IMPACT

Are we assessing economic contribution or economic impact? We must understand which concept a study is measuring in order to correctly interpret the results. These results are used to make government policy decisions and to determine business strategies. Therefore, it is important for economists and researchers to make sure the constructs they use have conceptual clarity.

Assumptions and Definitions

Economic Impact

Economic impact can be defined as "net changes in new economic activity associated with an industry, event, or policy in an existing regional economy context" (Watson et al., 2007). In the case studies that follow, economic impact is presented in terms of (1) business revenue, (2) value added or gross regional product, (3) personal income or wages and salaries, and (4) employment or jobs. These are indicators of improvement in the economic health of a region.

In determining the economic impact, we assume all changes due to a given industry are net new to the region, meaning changes are from outside sources or due to a previously uncaptured component. Such activities include exporting of goods and services by local businesses to areas outside the region, out-of-area visitor spending, and recapturing of economic activities sent outside the region due to a lack of local business services. For example, because less than one percent of surveyed Bonnaroo attendees originated in Coffee County, Tennessee, it is safe to assume that the music festival's impact is net new to the regional economy.

Economic Contribution

Watson et al. (2007) define economic contribution as a descriptive analysis that simply tracks the gross economic activity of the given event, policy, or industry as the dollars cycle through the region's economy. "This type of model is built to represent the structure and degree of interconnectedness in the regional economy with the output of each sector broken down and attributed to expenditures on intermediate inputs or to value-added components such as labor, taxes, and returns to capital" (Christophersen, Nadreau, and Olanie). A great example of this approach is in chapter 5: "Non-Profit Sector and the Regional Economy." In this case, the economic contribution refers to total spending of the nonprofit sector in the local economy. Because it is a broader concept, any measure of economic contributions includes the economic impact measures as well.

It is important in analyzing the role of an event or industry in a region that the concept of *economic contribution* be clearly separated from the concept of *economic impact*. In the case studies that follow, this distinction was clearly made. In the areas in which there are close *substitutes* to the event or organization within a region, it is better to call the aggregate impact *economic contribution* rather than *economic impact*. However, we must also acknowledge that the line is not always as clearly defined as it seems.

COST-BENEFIT ANALYSIS

CBA is used to assess the advantages and disadvantages of various projects. It is often used to assess net contributions of a public policy project to a community after taking into consideration the opportunity cost of the money invested.

According to Hanley and Spash (1993), "In any CBA, several steps should be conducted. These include: defining the project, identifying economically relevant impacts, physically quantifying impacts, and calculating a monetary evaluation." Chapter 6 in this book presents a step-by-step CBA of an infrastructure investment in a rural Tennessee region. The chapter begins with a set of assumptions driving the costs and benefits associated with port construction in a rural county. A comprehensive assessment of net present values of future costs and benefits associated with the project follows.

COUNTERFACTUAL ANALYSIS

The counterfactual approach removes the entire organization, industry, or event from the economy and then measures the economic impact or contribution of that subtraction. The advantage of using the counterfactual approach is the ability to measure the impact of an established organization, industry, or event.

In some cases an organization, industry, or event may have existed in a region for more than a century. In order to measure its impact, we must remove it from the baseline economy. We then take the difference between the baseline economy and the new equilibrium level after removal of the organization, industry, or event and its related activities.

SURVEY DATA VERSUS SECONDARY DATA ANALYSIS

The case studies that follow use survey data, secondary data, or both. "Surveys can come in many forms; they may be a series of questions asked face-to-face by interview, over the telephone, by mail, or by interactive communications" (Alvarez, Canduela, and Raeside, 2012). The five cases included in this book present a variety of ways to conduct and use survey methods in economic and fiscal assessment studies. For example, in the higher education study, the survey is used to capture broader interactions between business and higher education. In the Bonnaroo Music and Arts Festival study, the field surveys were the primary data source used to estimate the economic impact of the event on Coffee County.

Alvarez, Canduela, and Raeside (2012) cite that accuracy, relevancy, timeliness, accessibility, clarity, coherence, and completeness are the dimensions that need to be maximized in developing a survey. These principles guided the creation of the surveys used in the case studies. Secondary data is defined by Tripathy (2013) as "the use of existing research data to find answers to a question that was different from the original work. Secondary data can be a large scale survey or data collection as a part of personal research." When using secondary data, we assume the data has been "appropriately measured, validated, defined, and selected" (Johnson et al., 2009). As an extra measure to ensure data validity, case studies primarily use government-published or widely recognized data sets. An advantage of using secondary data is that "it saves lots of time, money, and other resources. Also data from large sample surveys may be of higher quality and more representative of the population" (Tripathy, 2013). Whenever resources and time allow, it is important to use surveys in addition to comprehensive secondary data collection in creating economic and fiscal assessments in a regional context.

INPUT-OUTPUT MODELS

Using input-output models to estimate indirect and induced effect of an event or industry is a common approach among applied regional economists and business and economic consultants. This is usually one of the final steps in assessing the economic and fiscal effect of an event or industry on a regional economy. Once you understand the challenge or business problem, frame the question, develop a conceptual framework, and collect both primary and secondary data, what is the next step? It is time to choose an economic model to assess the ripple effect. Economic impact studies often use one of the following three economic impact programs: Regional Economic Impact Modeling Inc. (REMI, http://www.remi.com); Impact Analysis for Planning (IMPLAN, http://www.implan.com); and Bureau of Economic Analysis regional multipliers (RIMS II, www.bea.gov). All five case studies in this book use the IMPLAN model to calculate indirect and induced effect of the institution, industry cluster, new investment, or music festival.

"Input-Output tables are used to develop multipliers which can be used to estimate the economic impacts of incremental spending in an economy" (Plumstead). The IMPLAN model includes procedures for generating multipliers and estimating impacts by applying final demand changes to the model. Direct effects are changes due to the first round of spending. Indirect effects are changes as a result of business-to-business transactions in the region. Induced effects are increases in sales within the region from employee spending within a given industry.

REGIONAL CONTEXT

Important factors to take into consideration when deciding which economic method to utilize are study area size and policy implications. The size of the study area affects the scope of contributions within an industry. "If a study area has a large, broad and diverse local economy it is likely that it will have the ability to retain these revenues longer as there are more opportunities for households and industries to purchase goods and services from local suppliers" (Watson et al., 2007).

After choosing an input-output model, the final step in the process is to create a customized region to assess the effect of an event or organization on this customized region. The region selected should make sense given the scope of an event. For example, Bonnaroo Music and Arts Festival takes place in Coffee County. Given the nature of this festival, it is not appropriate to use a state model to assess its impact on the county. A model customized for that specific county should be the one to use when assessing the economic impact of the festival on Coffee County. Using a large area to calculate the impact of an event on a smaller region overestimates the indirect and induced effects.

The case studies in this book present rich details on these issues. Each case begins with a problem statement, constructs a conceptual framework, defines the key concepts used in the case, specifies underlying assumptions that will

Table 2.1 An Overview of Analyses

	Health Care	Higher Education	Nonprofit Sector	Port at Cates Landing	Bonnaroo Music Festival
Counterfactual Analysis	◊	◊	◊		
Cost-Benefit Analysis				◊	
Survey Data vs. Secondary Data	Hybrid	Hybrid	Hybrid	Secondary	Survey
Input-Output Model	◊	◊	◊	◊	◊
Regional Context	Nashville MSA	Middle Tennessee Region/ Nashville MSA	Nashville MSA	Three Counties	Coffee County

Source: Table created by author

guide the process, selects an appropriate input-output model, and creates a customized regional model appropriate for the event, organization, or industry. Table 2.1 above summarizes the five chapters in relation to the concepts discussed here.

Chapter 3

Health Care Industry Cluster and Regional Economy

INTRODUCTION

Health care is a growth industry that is relatively immune to economic cycles. The health care sector has been the only sector consistently adding jobs throughout the worst economic crisis in recent history. Historical employment data and recent Bureau of Labor Statistics (BLS, www.bls.gov) surveys indicate that the basic health care services sector is driving employment growth in the national economy. Considering the health care worker shortage across the United States, it is likely that this growth trend will continue. Moreover, the baby boomer generation is expected to increase the demand for health care services over the years further increasing the demand for health care workers. Population projections from the Census Bureau suggest that the share of seniors (age 65 and over) in total population will increase to nearly 20 percent by 2030, up from 13 percent in 2010.

Amid overall growth in the health care sector throughout the United States, Nashville provides a unique example of a national health care industry hub. Fifty-six major health care companies (public and private) have chosen Nashville as their home, and seven of the nation's 12 leading for-profit acutecare hospital companies are located in Nashville, controlling more than one-third of investor-owned hospitals in the United States.[1]

The scope of the health care industry in Nashville ranges from basic-service providers such as physicians to more advanced biomedical research. This study presents two views of Nashville's health care industry: (1) the core health care industry, defined as ambulatory services, hospitals, and nursing and residential care facilities, and (2) the health care industry cluster, which encompasses the core health care industry and other related health care industries including management companies and health information technology.

This approach is necessary because the presence and quality of both components profoundly affect the region's economic status, business infrastructure, and quality of life.

Through a variety of methods, this study examines the reasons Nashville has become a salient locus in the national health care industry and analyzes the trends and scope of the core health care industry in Nashville from a comparative perspective. In addition, it provides a detailed assessment of the economic impact of the health care industry cluster on the regional economy. Furthermore, the study profiles the member companies of the NHCC and presents the *CEO Confidence Survey*. Finally, it presents a benchmarking initiative that compares Nashville with 12 peer Metropolitan Statistical Areas (MSAs) using a host of selected health care–related indicators. This study is a detailed analysis of the Nashville MSA, which includes Cannon, Cheatham, Davidson, Dickson, Hickman, Macon, Robertson, Rutherford, Smith, Sumner, Trousdale, Williamson, and Wilson counties. Wherever Nashville is mentioned in the study, it refers to the entire Nashville MSA. From a variety of sources, these data allows the Business and Economic Research Center (BERC) at Middle Tennessee State University to accurately determine the reasons Nashville has become a focal point in the national health care industry, assess the relationship between the health care industry and other sectors of the regional economy, and address other questions concerning Nashville's health care industry.

The rest of this study is organized as follows. First, we present an overview of trends in the core health care industry—comprising ambulatory services, hospitals, and nursing and residential care facilities—in the nation, Tennessee, and the Nashville MSA. Second, we briefly deal with the study's goals and methodology. Third, we put trends in the core health care industry in the Nashville MSA under close scrutiny exploring various aspects and growth dynamics of this industry. Furthermore, we highlight the importance of publicly traded health care management companies in Nashville's economy. Fourth, we adopt a broader view of the health care industry and assess the scope, size, and impact of the health care industry cluster on Nashville's economy. Fifth, we compare Nashville's core health care industry with that of 12 of its peer MSAs. Sixth, we explore survey results from NHCC member companies and presents the results of the CEO Confidence Survey.

OVERVIEW OF THE CORE HEALTH CARE INDUSTRY

The concept of the core health care industry refers to health care service providers classified as such under the NAICS (North American Industrial

Classification System): 621 (Ambulatory Services), 622 (Hospitals), and 623 (Nursing and Residential Care Facilities).

National Trends

Concerning national trends, increasing demand for health care services by the retiring baby boomer generation likely will fuel further growth in core health care industry employment. According to Census Bureau population projections, the percent of people over age 65 will increase to nearly 20 percent by 2030 from 13 percent in 2010.

Nationally, the core health care industry has grown significantly faster than nonfarm employment in the past 13 years. Core health care industry employment grew more than 10 percent between 2004 and 2008, while total nonfarm employment recorded a 4 percent growth rate. Nonfarm employment excluding health care grew nearly 4 percent in the same period. In addition, the health care industry's share in total employment increased 6 percent making its share in total employment almost 10 percent.

To give a better perspective on changing employment dynamics in the nation, one in 14 jobs created between 1995 and 2000 was in the health care sector. This has changed dramatically in recent years, as one in 4 jobs created between 2004 and 2008 was in the health care sector.

The growth trend in employment in the health care sector since 2000 is expected to continue through 2018, when core health care industry employment is projected to be the dominant source of employment growth. Health care occupations are projected to add nearly 2.8 million new jobs nationally between 2008 and 2018. In this period, growth in health care occupations is expected to be 24 percent versus 10 percent for all occupations. By 2018, health care occupations' share in total employment is projected to be 9 percent, nearly a percentage-point increase from 2008. Health care occupations will account for one in every six new jobs, and the resulting 2.8 million additional workers will be spread throughout this large and diverse sector from health care practitioners' offices, outpatient clinics and hospitals, to nursing and residential care facilities.[2]

According to the Bureau of Labor Statistics and the U.S. Department of Labor, three health care occupations are projected to be in the top 10 fastest-growing occupations in the U.S. These occupations include home health aides, physician assistants, and athletic trainers. Collectively, these occupations are projected to increase an average of 42 percent and add over 500,000 jobs between 2006 and 2016. Furthermore, The Center for Medicare and Medicaid expects national health care expenditures to reach $4.7 trillion by 2019 representing nearly 19 percent of gross domestic product (GDP), up from 16 percent in 2008.

Among national health care sectors, growth in ambulatory services outpaced growth in both nursing care facilities and hospital employment. Hospital and nursing care facilities employment grew 24 percent and 31 percent, respectively, while ambulatory services recorded 50 percent growth between 1995 and 2008.

The share of ambulatory services in total national health care employment increased considerably over the past 13 years. For example, ambulatory services accounted for 38 percent of total health care employment, nursing and residential care facilities 24 percent, and hospitals 38 percent in 1995. From 1995 to 2008, the share of ambulatory services employment grew (increasing to 42 percent) primarily at the expense of hospital employment which declined to 35 percent in 2008.

Trends in Tennessee

Tennessee's health care sector demonstrated significant resilience after a slow growth period between 1995 and 2000. Nonetheless, core health care employment grew nearly 16 percent between 2004 and 2008. In the same period, nonfarm employment grew substantially less, just 3 percent.

From a historical perspective, employment growth in Tennessee shows a reversal of trends between total nonfarm and health care employment. From 1995 to 2000, nonfarm employment showed a rigorous growth trend of nearly 10 percent versus a mere 5 percent for health services employment. However, this early growth pattern changed dramatically. From 2000 to 2004, health services employment grew nearly 14 percent versus nearly a 1 percent decline in total nonfarm. While the growth in health services employment continued to accelerate from 2004 to 2008, increasing nearly 16 percent, total nonfarm employment recorded an increase of only 3 percent, which corresponds to an annual average growth rate of less than 1 percent.

The growing share of seniors in the total population is likely to increase the demand for health care services drastically. According to Census Bureau projections, the share of old-age population (age 65 and over) in Tennessee's adult population is expected to increase from 13 percent in 2010 to more than 19 percent in 2030.

Although only three out of the 10 fastest-growing occupations in Tennessee are in health care, health care occupations are projected to increase 24 percent from 2006 to 2016.[3] Compared to the 12 percent growth in all occupations, health care occupations' share in total employment will increase to nearly 9 percent in 2016, up from 8 percent in 2006. Overall, health care occupations are projected to add 56,980 new jobs, accounting for one in every seven projected jobs between 2006 and 2016. Findings from Projection Central (www.projectioncentral.com) suggest that pharmacy technicians, orthodontists and prosthetists, and home health aides will be the fastest-growing health care occupations and part of the top 10 fastest-growing occupations statewide. These three jobs are expected to grow 57 percent, 45 percent, and 45 percent respectively. Together, they will add 9,520 new jobs in Tennessee.

In Tennessee, unlike the U.S. as a whole, the growth in health care employment was primarily driven by residential and nursing care facilities between 1995 and 2008; the nursing care facilities sector grew markedly faster than the other two health care sectors: ambulatory services and hospitals. Residential and nursing care facilities grew more than 44 percent while ambulatory services recorded a growth rate of 39 percent. Hospitals grew at a much slower pace than the other two health care segments with a growth rate of 34 percent.

Despite the increase in nursing and residential care employment, its share has remained stagnant at 19 percent between 1995 and 2008. Ambulatory services increased its employment share one percentage point from 1995 to 2008 at the expense of hospital employment.

Trends in the Nashville MSA

Nashville's health care employment grew faster than total nonfarm employment between 1995 and 2008. While nonfarm employment recorded a 3 percent growth rate between 2000 and 2004, Nashville's health care employment recorded a 25 percent growth rate during the same period. Albeit small, this growth trend continued between 2004 and 2008 when the nation was moving into its worst recession in recent history. During that period, Nashville's health care sector recorded a 15 percent growth rate.

From a historical perspective, Nashville's health care sector grew 54 percent from 1995 to 2008, adding more than 30,000 jobs. In this period, for every 100 nonfarm jobs, 22 were in health care. The period between 2000 and 2004 was the pinnacle of Nashville's health care sector, which added nearly 16,000 jobs; for every 100 nonfarm jobs created during this time, 92 were in the health care sector. Between 2004 and 2008, for every 100 nonfarm jobs, 26 were in the health care sector.

In line with national and state population growth trends, the Tennessee Advisory Commission on Intergovernmental Relations expects the share of seniors in Davidson County's adult population to reach 16 percent in 2025, up from 12 percent in 2010. Health care occupations in Nashville represented 9 percent of total jobs, or one in every 12 occupations, in 2008. In terms of the share of health care sector, one in every eight workers was employed by the health care industry.

In terms of changing employment dynamics by sector, nursing care employment increased about 6 percent from 2004. The increase in hospital and ambulatory services employment between 2004 and 2008 was phenomenal: 27 percent and 21 percent, respectively. Hospitals' share in health care jobs jumped nearly two percentage points to 46 percent in 2008.

Comparative Perspective on Trends in the Core Health Care Industry

Employment growth in Nashville's core health care industry has been faster than that of national and state health care employment since 2002. From 1995 to 2002, Nashville's health care employment was growing faster than Tennessee's health care employment but still slower than the United States. However in 2002, Nashville health care employment showed significant growth surpassing the trend for Tennessee and the United States in health care employment. During this time, from 2002 to 2008, Nashville health care employment grew nearly 30 percent versus 23 percent for Tennessee and 15 percent for the United States.

The core health care sector plays a more prominent role in Nashville's economy than in the state and national economies. More than 12 of every 100 Nashville nonfarm jobs in 2008 were core health care jobs.

The share of health care employment in total nonfarm employment for the Nashville MSA has consistently been nearly two percentage points greater than the shares in the United States and Tennessee. Similarly, it also follows the same trends during times of growth and reduction. The period between 1995 and 2000 shows a decrease in the percent share of health care employment in total nonfarm employment across all geographical units. In contrast, from 2000 to 2008, Nashville showed a significant increase in the percent share of health care employment. Employment in the health care sector rose from 9 percent in 2000 to over 12 percent in 2008. Tennessee and the United States have shown similar growth trends, but not as large. In 2000, Tennessee and the United States health care employment held an 8 percent share in total nonfarm employment. Ten percent was their common share in 2008.

Not surprisingly, the period of reduction in the share of health care employment coincides with substantial health care spending cuts as a result of the 1997 Balanced Budget Act which affected Nashville, a national health care industry hub, more than both the state and the nation. However, Nashville reinvented itself and moved forward faster than the U.S. and Tennessee.

STUDY GOALS AND METHODOLOGY

Goals of the Study

The goals of this study are sixfold:

1. What are the trends, scope, and impact of the core health care industry and health care industry cluster on the regional economy?
2. What is the economic significance to the region of Nashville's health care headquartered companies?
3. How does Nashville's health care industry compare with the health-care-industry in 12 of its peer MSAs?
4. How does the Nashville MSA rank relative to its 12 peer MSAs in terms of selected health care indicators?
5. What is the economic significance of NHCC members on the regional economy?
6. What are the expectations of NHCC member company CEOs for the national and local economies?

A Review of Selected Literature

Given the importance of the health care industry in the national and regional economies, many studies have treated this sector as an instrument for fueling economic growth. According to a recent study, "Economic Contribution of the Healthcare Industry to the City of Seattle (2004)," one in every five jobs in Seattle is tied to the health care sector. Considering the increasing share of national health care expenditures in GDP, this study highlights the challenges and opportunities the explosive demand for health care services creates for businesses, government, and individuals.[4]

Because this industry seems impervious to business cycles, many regional studies have emerged that place the health care industry at the center of regional economic growth. For example, a recent study by Market Street Services, Inc., identified Nashville's health care industry cluster as a key industry cluster in the regional economy.[5] Many studies, however, examine the health care sector from a perspective that narrowly focuses on health care providers: ambulatory services, hospitals, and nursing and residential care facilities. These studies lack the necessary broader perspective—viewing health care providers as a core health care industry at the center of a health care industry cluster. Greater growth potential in the health care industry is expected to result from increasing interaction between the core health care industry and health care–related infrastructure industries such as health care management, health care finance, life sciences research, and others.

The cluster perspective allows for a clearer understanding of not only health care providers but also other industrial linkages to the core health care industry and their combined economic impact on a regional economy. The Seattle study is a good example of the cluster treatment applied to the economic impact of the health care industry on a regional economy. A 2001 study of the health care industry in Louisville also presents the health care issue from a broader perspective that provides interindustry linkages as well as a regional comparison.[6] The critical conclusion reached by the Louisville and Seattle studies, which apply the cluster perspective, is that life sciences and medical research play a substantial role in the development of the health care industry and consequently greatly affect the regional economy. This salient fact remained unnoticed by studies that focused solely on health care providers without taking into consideration industrial linkages.

Missing from such presentations of the health care industry cluster is the growing role of health care management and health care services companies in the health care industry cluster. A classic example of the importance of management companies is seen in the growth of the health care industry in Nashville where accumulated knowledge of health care management and entrepreneurship is a foundation for innovations and breakthroughs that fuel the ever-changing national health care industry landscape. A brief history of Nashville's health care industry attests to this fact (NHCC). Therefore, this study includes health care management companies as part of the health care industry cluster.

Method and Data

Indicators for this study are collected from different sources. It is often difficult to find comparable figures for the peer MSAs due to data suppression. BERC used a multitude of different sources to estimate comparable figures for these MSAs. This analysis is guided by the availability of data for health care–related indicators. Throughout this study, there may be some slight discrepancies in figures due to the estimation methods used by different employment surveys. BERC consulted several sources to construct a time-series perspective on health care indicators for Nashville and the peer MSAs.

Selection of MSAs

In consultation with the NHCC and the Nashville Area Chamber of Commerce, BERC has identified 12 peer MSAs for Nashville: Atlanta, Birmingham, Charlotte, Columbus, Dallas, Denver, Indianapolis, Jacksonville, Kansas City (MO), Louisville, Raleigh, and Richmond, all major U.S. MSAs with substantial health care–related economic activity. BERC's selection of these MSAs was also guided by the literature (e.g., see Coomes and Narang, 2001).

Survey Method

Since 1995, NHCC has promoted the growth of the health care industry in Nashville. NHCC has a unique member mix in that both health care and professional services (i.e., management, information technology, finance, and law) companies work together to forge strong ties to accelerate growth in the health care industry. BERC conducted a survey to develop a profile of NHCC member companies.

Definitions

Throughout this study, BERC classifies Nashville's health care industry into three distinct categories: (1) core health care industry, (2) health care industry cluster, and (3) NHCC member companies. Figure 3.1 indicates the relationship between these three categories of health care industry classification.

Conceptual Framework for Impact Analysis

The economic impact assessment of the health care industry is based on the health care industry cluster definition previously provided. The goal of this assessment is to highlight what happens if the entire health care industry cluster is removed from the regional economy. BERC reports the direct, indirect, and induced economic impact of counterfactually removing the health care industry cluster from the economy.[7] The report presents three categories of impact: output, employment, and personal income. For each of these categories, BERC also reports leakages out of Nashville and the relationship between the health care industry cluster and other sectors of the economy. BERC made adjustments to the indirect and induced effects

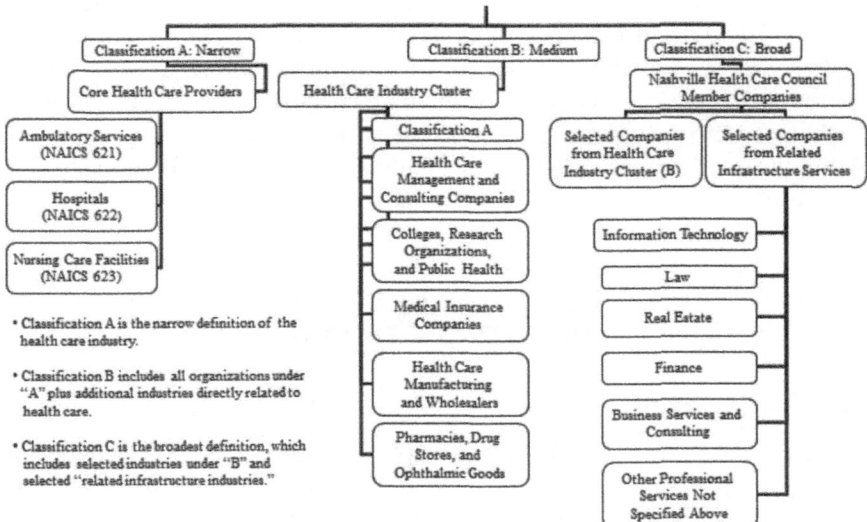

Figure 3.1 Health Care Industry Classification in this Study. *Source*: Figure created by author

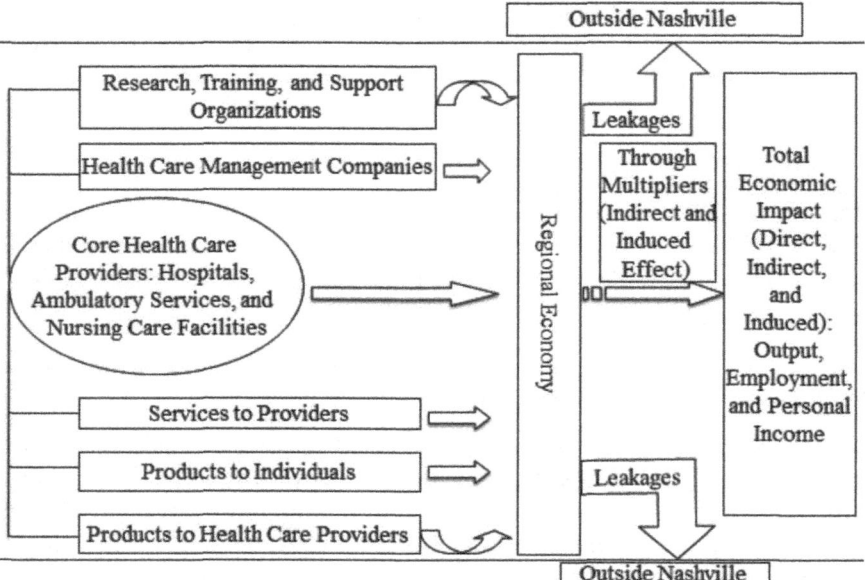

Figure 3.2 Conceptual Framework for Impact Analysis. *Source*: Figure created by author

of the health care subsectors on each other within the health care industry cluster. BERC assumes that IMPLAN (see appendix) regional purchasing coefficients (RPC) represent the current situation, and the differences between 100 percent local purchase and the default model RPCs determine the leakages outside of Nashville. To avoid double counting, the core health care providers were not allowed to stimulate the health care sector and other subsectors in the cluster. Figure 3.2 shows the conceptual framework that highlights the procedure used to calculate the economic impact of the health care cluster.

CORE HEALTH CARE INDUSTRY IN NASHVILLE: ITS SCOPE AND TREND

Total Employment

Nashville's core health care sector employs just over 90,000 people, up more than 22 percent from 2004. By segment, 38 percent are in ambulatory services, 46 percent in hospitals, and 16 percent in nursing care facilities.[8] The core health care sector includes NAICS 621, 622, and 623. The share of hospital employment increased more than 2 percentage points between the years 2004 and 2008 reversing the trend for years 2001 to 2004.

Each segment of the Nashville MSA core health care industry experienced phenomenal growth over both the long and short terms. From 2001 to 2008, ambulatory services grew nearly 42 percent, hospitals 37 percent, and nursing care 17 percent. In the short run, between 2004 and 2008, hospitals experienced a nearly one-third increase in employment, followed by ambulatory services with 21 percent growth and nursing care with 8 percent. Core health care employment in the Nashville MSA has increased 35 percent from 2001 to 2008 showing a majority of growth between 2004 and 2008.

Employment by Occupation

A salient difference between employment in the health care sector and employment by health care occupations is that the former includes all occupations in the sector ranging from accountant to medical doctor. However, health care occupations refer to medical professionals and allied health occupations and do not include occupations in health care education and research. Nonetheless, health care occupations account for about 8 percent of total occupations in the Nashville MSA. Overall, average wage for health care occupations at $51,731 is significantly higher than Nashville's average annual wage of $39,280.

Sectoral Diversity

The health services sector (the core health care industry) is the third largest in Nashville's economy, after government and professional and business services, representing 12 percent of total nonfarm jobs. This is a significant improvement from 2004 when it ranked fifth after manufacturing and retail trade.[9] A significant jump from 2004, more than 15 percent, made the sector a pillar of Nashville's economy.

In this context, we would like to briefly address the perennial issue of which sector ranks first in the Nashville MSA. In evaluating this issue, we would like to emphasize that employment is only one aspect of an economic sector's contribution to the regional economy: business revenue, value added, personal income, and indirect business taxes are additional, often overlooked considerations. Table 3.1 is a simple guide for those interested in the full picture of an economic sector's role in a region's economy.

As demonstrated, employment is only one measure of the effect of economic activities on a region's economy. Although its ranking by employment is behind other sectors, manufacturing is still number one in terms of creating

Chapter 3

Table 3.1   Contribution to Nashville's Economy by Sector

	Employment		Business Revenue		Value Added (GDP)		Cumulative Ranking	
	Score	Rank	Score	Rank	Score	Rank	Average Score	Final Rank
Mining, Logging, and Construction	0.27	8	0.33	9	0.19	10	0.26	9
Manufacturing	0.68	6	1.00	1	0.96	1	0.88	1
Wholesale	0.25	9	0.42	6	0.52	6	0.40	8
Retail	0.82	4	0.41	7	0.51	7	0.58	6
Transportation and Utilities	0.18	11	0.33	10	0.25	9	0.25	10
Information	0.12	12	0.27	11	0.17	11	0.19	11
Financial Activities	0.34	7	0.62	3	0.84	3	0.60	5
Professional and Business Services	0.91	2	0.61	4	0.81	4	0.78	3
Educational Services	0.11	13	0.20	13	0.10	13	0.14	13
Health and Social Assistance	0.86	3	0.63	2	0.87	2	0.78	2
Leisure and Hospitality	0.75	5	0.36	8	0.31	8	0.47	7
Other Services	0.19	10	0.22	12	0.11	12	0.17	12
Government	0.92	1	0.47	5	0.77	5	0.72	4

Source: Table created by author

economic value in the region. Overall, health care ranks second and professional and business services third.

Establishments

Ambulatory services account for almost 90 percent of establishments (a single business location of a company) in the core health care industry. Since 2001, ambulatory services establishments have grown nearly 28 percent. Nursing care facilities and hospitals account for about 10 percent of establishments. Their respective growths between 2001 and 2008 are 41 percent and 13 percent. Together, the core health care sector added 600 new establishments between 2001 and 2008 with 81 percent of the new establishments being added between 2001 and 2004.

Wages

In 2008, wages in the core health care industry in Nashville totaled $4.7 billion with hospitals and ambulatory services accounting for 92 percent of those wages. Moreover, total wages across core health care industry segments increased between 2004 and 2008: hospital wages increased from $1.49 billion to $2.45 billion; ambulatory services wages increased from $1.43 billion to $1.87 billion; and nursing care facilities wages rose from $0.34 billion to $0.39 billion. Of the three health care industry segments, hospitals experienced the greatest increase in total wages, 64 percent. Ambulatory services wages increased 31 percent and nursing care 15 percent.

Historically, Nashville's health care sector commands wages higher than average nonfarm wages. According to this trend, the gap between health care and nonfarm wages is far from closing. In fact, the current wage gap on average is more than $10,000. The average wage for Nashville's health care sector in 2008 was $52,160. Given the average nonfarm wage of $39,280, this translates into a wage gap of more than $12,000.

Export Potential of Core Health Care Industry Segments

Location quotient (LQ) is often used to describe the relationship between the local and national economies. If the LQ for an industry is larger than 1, that industry has a larger presence in the local economy than its national economic counterpart. Hospitals and ambulatory services employ substantially more people in the Nashville MSA than in the U.S. Consequently, these findings suggest that supply in the region exceeds local demand for hospitals and ambulatory services, and that these health care establishments serve residents outside the Nashville area. These industries hold a LQ of 1.56 and 1.04, respectively. In the case of nursing care, LQ .84, Nashville area residents are most likely to use long-term care services outside the local economy.

Relative Growth Performance of Core Health Care Segments

The health care and social services sector grew faster than other sectors in the Nashville MSA. Growth in health care and social services was substantially

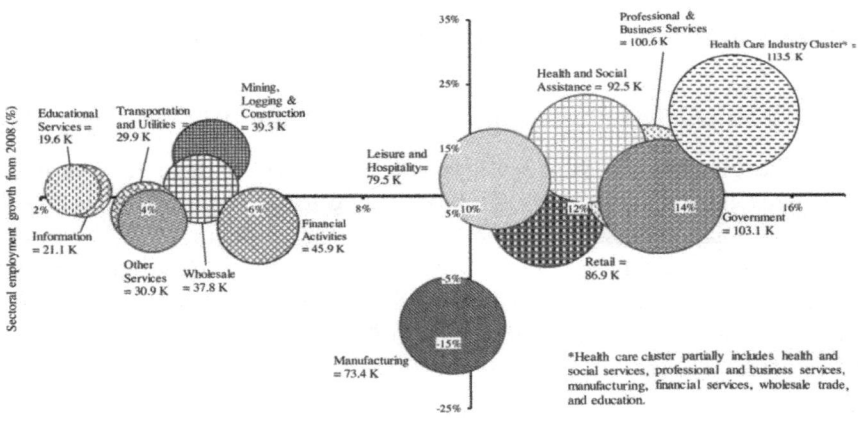

Figure 3.3 "Core Health Care Industry" Trend in Nashville: Relative Performance from 2004 to 2008 (Bubbles show the actual employment level of each aggregated sector).
Source: Figure created by author

Table 3.2 Where Does $1 Million in Core Industry Spending Go in the Local Economy? (Major Industries Only)

Industry	Value	Percent
Services to buildings	$4,645	0.46
Other basic organic chemical manufacturing	$4,665	0.47
Office administrative services	$4,884	0.49
Postal service	$5,774	0.58
Management consulting services	$6,319	0.63
Power generation and supply	$6,533	0.65
Surgical and medical instrument manufacturing	$6,894	0.69
Plastic, plumbing fixtures, and all other plastics	$6,930	0.69
Management of companies and enterprises	$7,657	0.77
Food services and drinking places	$8,044	0.80
Other ambulatory health care services	$9,401	0.94
Legal services	$9,742	0.97
Securities-commodity contracts-investments	$10,795	1.08
Wholesale trade	$10,878	1.09
Employment services	$11,995	1.20
Pharmaceutical and medicine manufacturing	$13,099	1.31
Real estate	$46,040	4.60
Other sectors	$106,798	10.68
Institutions/Individuals		
Employee compensation	$383,057	38.31
Proprietary income	$255,646	25.56
Other property income	$70,934	7.09
Indirect business taxes	$9,270	0.93
Total	$1,000,000	100

Source: Table created by author.

larger than the average sector growth rate of 6 percent. Furthermore, its current share in total employment is 5 percent above the average for all sectors.

Core Health Care Industry and the Local Economy

More than 70 percent of core health care spending goes to institutions or individuals as either payroll or proprietary income in the Nashville MSA. Real estate, pharmaceuticals, employment services, wholesale trade, and securities investment are the top five sectors that benefit most from the business expenditures of health care companies in Nashville. These calculations are based on the assumption that all spending occurs in the local economy.

NASHVILLE'S HEALTH CARE INDUSTRY CLUSTER

In order to measure the economic impact of Nashville's health care industry cluster, BERC uses the counterfactual approach. This differs from the net new concept, in that the counterfactual approach removes the whole health care industry cluster from the economy, and then measures the total economic impact that the subtraction generates across the remaining economy. Besides the counterfactual approach, BERC also uses employment by sector as an input when assessing the economic impact of the health care industry cluster. Finally, in the absence of detailed industry spending by zip code and vendor, BERC uses default RPC to allow for outside leakage. Then, BERC treats the outside leakages as the difference between the impact results with the default RPC and the impact results with 100 percent local purchasing.

BERC assumes that each group of sectors in the health care industry cluster is not only closely linked to the core health care sector but that each sector also has its own independent effect on the local economy. Therefore, BERC measures the economic impact of the individual groups of sectors independent of each other and then adjusts the measure of the economic impact to take into consideration the indirect impact of group on the core health care sector and vice versa.

When the health care industry cluster is removed from the economy, BERC assumes that an economic shock to the core health care providers should not have a ripple effect on itself. An adjustment for this purpose has been made to the study results.

In this study, BERC reports on the direct, indirect, and induced impacts of the Nashville health care industry cluster. The direct impact refers to the current state of employment, sales, and personal income generated by the cluster in an economy. The indirect impact refers to the employment, sales, and personal income generated in the local economy by a business-to-business transaction. For example, a hospital purchases goods and services from local businesses for its operation. This hospital's spending in the local economy means additional jobs, business revenues, and personal income in other sectors. Induced impact refers to the employment, sales, and personal income generated in the local economy by employee spending.

For example, a hospital employs and pays many individuals for their work at the hospital. These workers then spend their earnings in the local economy to maintain their lifestyle. This process generates additional jobs, business revenues, and personal income across the local economy. Finally, BERC also estimates linkages between the health care industry cluster and other sectors in the local economy.

Employment and Office Space

The Nashville health care industry cluster employs 113,453 people (2008), which corresponds to 15 of every 100 nonfarm employees in Nashville. Nashville health care industry cluster employment increased 20 percent from

2004. As an industry cluster, its employment is the largest among major aggregate sectors in the Nashville MSA. Additionally, the Nashville health care cluster accounts for nearly 31 million square feet of office space, up 19 percent from 2004, which corresponds to 16 percent of Nashville's total office and industrial space.[10]

The Nashville health care industry cluster is divided into six major segments of health care: management and consulting, research, training and support organizations, services to providers, products to individuals, and health care providers, at the core. Of these six major sectors, health care providers (NAICS 621,622, 623) hold an 80 percent share of employment and a 71 percent share of office space in the total of all employment and office space in the Nashville health care industry cluster. The remaining 20 percent of employees are split between the five other sectors, of which health care management and consulting organizations have the largest share with 9,604 employees.

Establishments and Wages

The Nashville health care industry cluster, consisting of nearly 3,600 establishments, accounts for $6.02 billion in wages. From 2004 to 2008, the number of establishments increased nearly 9 percent, while the cluster wages increased 40 percent over the same period. Average health care cluster wage is estimated at $52,773 in 2008. This average wage is significantly higher than Nashville's average nonfarm wage of $39,280. Nashville's health care cluster average wage increased about 16 percent from 2004.

Like the previous segment, health care providers account for $4.7 billion in wages, 78 percent, and 2,703 establishments, 75 percent. The remaining $1.3 billion is wages spent between the five other major sectors with health care management and consulting paying over $653 million. On the other hand, the remaining 879 establishments are split between the other sectors. Products to individuals hold 393, or 45 percent, of the remaining establishments.

Investor-Owned Health Care Management Companies (Public and Private)

Many studies examine the locational patterns of large corporate headquarters in the U.S. The findings suggest that the presence of large corporate headquarters provides substantial benefits to the regional economy since such headquarters (1) bring high-paying jobs, (2) increase the competitive advantage of the host cities, (3) promote innovative technologies through acquisition and dissemination of information, and (4) spur growth in critical infrastructure industries, such as law, finance, and other professional and business services.[11]

Furthermore, the location decision of large corporate headquarters is also shaped by the presence of certain qualities in the host region, primarily (1) a good quality of life, (2) major transportation and communication infrastructure, (3) a diverse economic base, (4) a sound financial infrastructure, (5) professional services, and (6) a highly skilled labor force.

As an epicenter of corporate headquarters activities, Nashville presents a unique combination of these qualities. According to Klier and Testa's findings (2002), Nashville was one of the few large cities to experience phenomenal relocation of major corporate headquarters between 1990 and 2000. During this period, 16 large corporations chose Nashville as their new headquarters location for a growth rate of 178 percent. From 2006 to 2009, The Nashville Chamber of Commerce reports that more than 30 company headquarters have relocated to the Nashville MSA. Recently, MarketWatch's 2009 annual survey named the Nashville MSA as the 15th best city for business in the U.S. In addition, the April 2010 issue of *Site Selection* magazine named the Nashville Chamber's economic development team as one of the 10 best in the nation.

Nashville is truly the center of gravity for national health care industry company headquarters with 56 major public and private companies calling it home. Only companies with more than $500,000 in revenue and at least 100 employees are included in this analysis. As of 2009, 494 out of 958 investor-owned hospitals in the U.S. were owned or operated by Nashville area hospital management companies. In 2008, the 56 health care industry cluster companies headquartered in Nashville counted revenues of more than $62 billion and employed nearly 400,000 people worldwide.[12]

From a different perspective, seven of the top 12 investor-owned acute-care hospital companies are Nashville-based (www.hospitalreviewmagazine.com). These seven companies alone own and operate 384 acute care hospitals.[13] Nashville-based health care companies have been involved in substantial private equity flows in the U.S. An often-cited example is a 2006 HCA deal of more than $32 billion in private equity that has been cited as the largest private equity deal in health care.

Nashville is also a hub for publicly traded health care companies in the U.S. As of 2008, 17 such companies calling Nashville home had combined employment of more than 145,000 globally and combined revenue of nearly $26 billion. Table 3.3 is a profile of these publicly traded health care management companies as well as the largest investor-owned private companies. Together, they form a powerful worldwide presence in the Nashville health care industry cluster with $61 billion in business revenues and more than 375,000 employees. These companies represent, by far, the largest contributors to worldwide jobs and revenue among headquarters in Nashville's health care industry cluster.

Chapter 3

Table 3.3 Nashville-Based Investor-Owned Health Care Management Companies

Company Name	Ticker	No. of Employees	Sales/Revenue
HCA Inc.	Private	191,000	$28,374,000,000
Vanguard Health Systems	Private	17,100	$2,300,000,000
Iasis Healthcare LLC.	Private	10,775	$2,070,000,000
Ardent Health Services LLC.	Private	8,800	$1,800,000,000
Capella Healthcare Inc.	Private	2,700	$500,000,000
Cumberland Pharmaceuticals Inc.	CPIX	53	$43,500,000
Emdeon Inc.	EM	2,200	$853,600,000
Advocat Inc.	AVCA	2,809	$302,031,000
America Service Group Inc.	ASGR	4,100	$606,176,000
American Homepatient Inc.	AHOM	2,362	$236,297,000
Amsurg Corp	AMSG	1,630	$668,752,000
Biomimetic Therapeutics Inc.	BMTI	88	$3,148,384
Brookdale Senior Living Inc.	BKD	23,500	$2,023,068,000
Community Health Systems Inc.	CYH	55,579	$12,107,613,000
Healthcare Realty Trust Inc.	HR	229	$257,178,000
Healthspring Inc.	HS	1,800	$2,661,755,000
Healthstream, Inc.	HSTM	300	$57,389,000
Healthways, Inc.	HWAY	3,500	$717,426,000
Lifepoint Hospitals Inc.	LPNT	15,700	$2,962,700,000
National Health Investors Inc.	NHI	1	$70,127,000
National Healthcare Corp	NHC	12,000	$668,221,000
Psychiatric Solutions Inc.	PSYS	16,000	$1,805,361,000
Total	22	375,226	$61,088,351,384

Source: Table created by author

ECONOMIC IMPACT OF THE NASHVILLE HEALTH CARE CLUSTER

Employment Impact

The health care industry cluster's total employment impact is 211,059, which equals 8 percent of Tennessee's and 28 percent of the Nashville MSA's nonfarm employment in 2008. The breakdown of this impact is as follows: direct impact was 113,454 jobs. Indirect and induced impacts generated an additional 33,073 and 64,532 jobs, respectively. One hundred industry cluster jobs create an additional 86 jobs in the Nashville economy. The employment impact of Nashville's health care industry cluster increased 36 percent from 2004.

Sectoral Impact

The largest sectors impacted by the health care industry cluster are retail trade and administrative and waste management services with nearly 15,000 jobs each. Because of interregional transactions, Nashville's health care industry cluster creates 23,416 additional jobs across sectors outside Nashville.

Industry Linkages

As highlighted in the last section, the Nashville health care cluster is responsible for creating 97,605 jobs as a result of indirect and induced impacts. For every 1,000 health care industry cluster jobs created, an additional 129 jobs are created in retail trade and administrative services, 103 in real estate, 100 in accommodation, 89 in other services, 68 in finance, 32 in health and social services, and 29 in transportation.

Business Revenue Impact

The total business revenue impact of the health care industry cluster in 2008 is $29.2 billion, $16.8 billion of which is directly injected into the economy. Indirect and induced impacts add an extra $4.2 million and $8.2 million, respectively, to the regional economy. The business revenue impact of Nashville's health care industry cluster increased 60 percent from 2004. This amount is equivalent to nearly 6 percent of Tennessee's and 19 percent of Nashville's total business revenues in 2008. Every $100 in health care cluster spending generates an additional $74 in business revenues.

Sectoral Impact

The real estate and rental sector in Nashville greatly benefits from the health care industry cluster, garnering $3.1 billion in business revenues as a result. Sectors including finance and retail trade also benefit seeing $1.6 billion and $1.1 billion in leakages, respectively. Moreover, leakage outside of Nashville is $3.5 billion across sectors.

Industry Linkages

Every $1,000 in business revenue generated by the health care industry cluster generates additional revenues of $184 in real estate, $93 in finance, $64 in retail, and $56 in information. Other sectors seeing substantial benefits are administrative and waste management ($52), professional and business services ($41), and accommodation ($39). The impact on other sectors ranges from $38 in manufacturing to $1 in agriculture.

Personal Income

The Nashville health care industry cluster generates $13.4 billion in personal income for the local economy. This corresponds to 6 percent of Tennessee's and nearly 22 percent of the Nashville MSA's total personal income in 2008. Moreover, every $100 of personal income generates an additional $39 in the local economy. The personal income impact of Nashville's health care industry cluster increased 59 percent from 2004.

Sectoral Impact

The largest sectoral impact is in finance with $515 million. Other notable sectors benefiting from the Nashville health care industry cluster are administrative and waste services ($465 million), retail trade ($447 million), and professional and business services ($328 million). Total outside leakage is estimated at $1.7 billion across all sectors.

Industry Linkages

Every $1,000 in personal income earned in the health care industry cluster creates an additional $53 in finance, $48 in administrative and waste management, and $46 in retail trade. In addition, there are substantial impacts on professional services ($34), real estate ($32), other services ($26), and accommodation ($24). Finally, the impact on other sectors ranges from $19 in information to $0.05 in agriculture.

FISCAL IMPACT OF THE NASHVILLE HEALTH CARE INDUSTRY CLUSTER

The Nashville health care industry cluster accounts for $1.2 billion in state and local taxes. Of this amount, nearly half stems from sales tax while property tax, corporate dividends and profit taxes, and other taxes and fees make up the remainder. Compared to 2004, the fiscal impact of Nashville's health care industry cluster is up nearly 55 percent. From a comparative perspective, this figure represents more than 7 percent of all taxes collected in Tennessee and nearly 20 percent of all taxes collected in the Nashville MSA in 2008.

NASHVILLE'S CORE HEALTH CARE INDUSTRY FROM A COMPARATIVE PERSPECTIVE

Export Potential and Employment Growth

Indicators of health care employment suggest that the Nashville MSA has a strong health care industry presence compared to its peer MSAs. Health care employment per capita is the largest among the peers with 59 employees per

1,000 people. Similarly, employment share of the health care sector is the largest among the peers with 12 percent in 2008. Finally, in terms of growth of health care employment from 2004, all MSAs show a positive growth trend: the Nashville MSA ranks sixth with 15 percent.

Furthermore, the Nashville MSA's health care industry overall has the best export potential among 13 comparable MSAs. A score greater than one "1" (LQ > 1) suggests that a MSA is exporting health care services; that is, residents from other areas are traveling to the region to use its health care services. The Nashville MSA performed better than its peer MSAs in 2008 and also showed a positive growth trend with an increase of slightly over 1 percent from 2004.

Health Care Industry Cluster Headquarters and Global Impact

Nashville ranks first among the 13 MSAs in terms of number of major health care industry cluster management companies (both public and private), their revenues, and their employment. Although Nashville only has half of the number of health care cluster headquarters as Dallas, the number two ranked MSA, Nashville's total employment and revenues from those headquarters nearly double that of Dallas. Furthermore, Nashville's global impact is quite substantial with more than 400,000 jobs and $62 billion in annual business revenues generated by investor-owned health care management companies.[14]

Health Care Occupations

Nashville ranks second among the 13 MSAs in terms of percent of health care occupations in total occupations. The range of the share of health care occupations varies from Birmingham with 10 percent to Atlanta with 6 percent. Nashville ties with Columbus for second both having the share of 8 percent. Similar findings show Nashville ranks fourth among peer MSAs in terms of health care occupations per capita with 42 occupations per 1,000 people. This is 11 percent higher than the peer MSA's average of 38.

Although Nashville's average wage for health care occupations is $51,731, it is less than the average of its peers. However, it is relatively higher, 32 percent, than the average nonfarm wage. Additionally, Nashville ranks second in paying the largest difference from the average nonfarm wage among peer MSAs only falling behind Indianapolis with 33 percent.[15]

Venture Capital Flow

Tennessee ranks fourth among 12 states in terms of venture capital flow in medical devices, equipment, health services, and biotechnology. Ahead of Tennessee in terms of venture capital is North Carolina ranking number one and Texas ranking number two. As a whole, these 12 states account for nearly 15 percent of all venture capital flows in the U.S. in the past 11 years. Nashville contributed to nearly $1 billion in venture capital flows in the time between 1998 and 2009. This is comparable to North Carolina having the highest of all with $2.7 billion and Alabama contributing the lowest of the peer MSAs with $117 million.[16]

Total value of venture capital in Tennessee between 1998 and 2009 was $283 million in medical equipment, $578 million in health services, and $127 million in biotechnology. Tennessee's share of venture capital in health services in U.S. health services venture capital was three times the peer MSA average with 9 percent. Much of this amount flowed to the Nashville MSA. This assigns a clear leadership position to Nashville in access to funding for health care services companies. Across the medical equipment and biotechnology sectors, Nashville does not have as much as a crucial role. North Carolina and Texas hold the largest share of venture capital in medical equipment with 2 percent of the U.S. total. Nashville holds 1 percent in this category. Similarly, North Carolina also holds the greatest share in biotechnology with over 4 percent of the United States total. Tennessee is not a competitive force in this sector accounting for much less than the peer MSA average.

Where Does the Nashville MSA Stand Relative to Its Peers?

There are many studies for both academic and public policy purposes that analyze quality of life, business climate, infrastructure, and socioeconomic productivity across cities. While many of these studies are comprehensive in terms of their use of indicators and coverage area, some focus on a single issue, such as education.[17] The rankings serve many purposes: business groups use them as a marketing tool, policy-makers address the deficiencies in their respective regions, and individuals and businesses make their relocation decisions based on these rankings. From these perspectives, the rankings play an important role in understanding socioeconomic dynamics across regions.

A glance at various rankings demonstrates that Nashville is in the top 10 among comparable MSAs in terms of infrastructure and human capital.[18] Over the years, *Expansion Management* and *Business Facilities* magazines have ranked Nashville among the top metropolitan areas in which to do business, and Nashville has topped *Expansion Management*'s list of the 50 hottest cities for business expansion and relocation for two years consecutively in 2005 and 2006. Most recently, Tennessee has been ranked the 13th most business tax friendly state in 2010. Furthermore, Franklin, Tennessee, is ranked the eighth best city for startup companies.[19] Along similar lines, this study provides rankings of 13 comparable MSAs in the area of health care services.

This study uses two categories of ranking: health care business climate and health care infrastructure. For ranking purposes, BERC identified 14 indicators for the health care business climate and 21 for health care infrastructure.

Selection of indicators was affected by (1) availability of reliable data across peer MSAs and (2) literature on business climate and infrastructure indicators. Before rankings, each indicator was converted to a unitless relative score bounded between zero and one [0, 1]. These relative scores were then averaged across indicators for each MSA within the given category (business climate or infrastructure).

BERC's final rankings are based on two fundamental assumptions: (1) each indicator contributes equally to the final score for a given category (no weights are assigned to the indicators), and (2) each indicator's contribution to a given category is linear.

Health Care Business Climate Indicators

The health care business climate in Nashville is substantially better than in the 12 other MSAs. The Nashville MSA ranked first for six indicators: health care employment share (2008), health care employment per capita (2008), total private health care cluster headquarter employment (2000) and revenues, total public health care cluster headquarter employment (2000), and health care export capacity (2008). Five indicators also ranked Nashville either number two or three in comparison to peer MSAs. These indicators are: health care occupations per share and per capita (2008), number of private and public health care cluster headquarters (2009), and total public health care cluster headquarter revenues. In addition, 13 out of 14 indicators ranked the Nashville MSA above the average of its peers for their respective indicators.

Health Care Infrastructure Indicators

Health care infrastructure plays a smaller role in the Nashville MSA than the health care business climate, yet it is still competitive with its peer MSAs. Nashville ranked number one in the following four indicators: cost per dental visit (2006), health care cost index (2006), and venture capital and deals in health services at the state level (2004 to 2009). It also ranked number three for physicians per capita and change in economic diversity (2004 to 2008). Nashville also performed better than the average peer MSA in 10 out of 21 indicators.

Relative Rankings

In the health care business climate, the Nashville MSA ranks first among the 13 MSAs, while Indianapolis ranks second, Columbus third, and Richmond fourth. While Nashville maintained its rank from a similar ranking in 2005, Louisville's rank slipped from second to sixth. In health care infrastructure, similar to its ranking in 2005, Nashville ranks second after Indianapolis, followed by Dallas (third) and Jacksonville (fourth). Rankings of peer MSAs other than Nashville changed significantly in this category. Finally, in overall relative health care competitiveness, Nashville again tops the chart, while Indianapolis ranks second, Dallas third, Columbus fourth, and Richmond fifth. There is again a significant shift in ranking across peers.

NASHVILLE HEALTH CARE COUNCIL (NHCC) MEMBER COMPANIES

Survey Methodology

The NHCC member companies are diverse ranging from direct health care providers and health care management, health information technology, and health care finance companies to such professional service providers as law and architecture firms. BERC's survey asked companies to report their health care–related employment, sales, office space, federal research money, payroll, and operating sites—both in Nashville and worldwide. Furthermore, the survey also included a CEO Confidence Survey, highlighting member company CEO's evaluation of current economic conditions and business outlook.

Because the NHCC member companies represent a diverse group, they differ from the previous two classifications of the health care industry presented in this report: core health care providers and health care industry cluster. Core health care providers narrowly define the sector and include only companies providing direct services to individuals. The health care industry cluster includes health care providers plus companies directly linked to the core providers sector. NHCC member companies are more diverse than the previous two classifications in terms of the industry segment. Readers should review this study with these salient differences between the three groups in mind.

As of November 2009, NHCC had 170 member companies, a 53 percent increase from 2005. BERC conducted an online survey of NHCC member companies with follow-up reminders from NHCC. The survey included three parts: (1) company profile, (2) company operations, and (3) CEO Confidence Survey. A total of 149 member companies were invited to fill out the survey. Twenty-one companies were excluded from the process since they did not have an employment base in the Nashville MSA. Consequently, 65 companies responded to parts 1 and 2 of the survey for a response rate of 44 percent. BERC estimated the 84 missing company figures using company databases (e.g., ReferenceUSA, LexisNexis Academic Universe), individual member company websites, and other sources. Through these methods of extrapolation, BERC prepared profiles for 149 member companies.

NHCC member survey response rate for business outlook was slightly better than for previous sections: BERC received responses from 70 businesses for a response rate of 47 percent. The CEO Confidence Survey was designed to include certain elements from the business confidence survey conducted quarterly by the Conference Board and the business outlook survey conducted monthly by the Federal Reserve Bank of Philadelphia.

NHCC Member Companies—Employment and Wages

Operating at 217 sites, NHCC member companies employ nearly 70,000 people in the Nashville MSA, up 70 percent from 2005. The total Nashville-based payroll is $4.9 billion, up 36 percent from 2005. The average payroll per employee is $70,015, substantially higher than the average nonfarm wage in the Nashville MSA. According to Bureau of Economic Analysis (www.bea.gov) figures, the average annual wage in the Nashville MSA in 2008 was $39,280. Considering the difference, NHCC member companies command substantial purchasing power in the Nashville MSA, which has profound implications for the local tax base. Many NHCC member companies are large corporate headquarters and health care management companies that employ highly skilled individuals who are experts in their respective fields. As previously discussed, these are some of the benefits that corporate headquarters bring to a region.

Unfortunately, this survey was not designed to address corporate citizenship of NHCC member companies. Many studies highlight the role of corporate citizenship in a community. Large companies, especially in health care, traditionally make substantial contributions to local charities, civic organizations, local governments, and individuals through direct cash donations, volunteer time, matching employee donations, in-kind contributions, and charity care.

More than one-third of the NHCC member companies employ less than 20 people in the Nashville MSA. A handful of large member companies employing over 1,000 people account for more than 60 percent of the NHCC members' local employment. A total of 61 member companies reported global employment. One-third of companies (those with over 1,000 headquarter employees) accounted for 96 percent of 374,111 global employees for the period between November 10, 2009, and January 15, 2010.

Not all of these jobs, however, are related to health care. For more than 36 percent of the NHCC member companies, health care is not their core business as fewer than 30 percent of their employees are related to health care. However, globally, NHCC member companies reported that 26 percent of employees were less than 30 percent health care related. Taking into account health care–related share of their employment, NHCC member companies have more than 64,000 health care–related employees in the Nashville MSA and nearly 262,000 globally.

NHCC member companies reported a total of $4.9 billion in wages and salaries in the Nashville MSA. Sixty-five percent of the companies have an annual payroll of less than $10 million accounting for 7 percent of the total payroll of NHCC member companies. The 55 companies with payrolls over $10 million account for 93 percent, or $4.6 billion dollars, in wages and salaries.

NHCC member companies reported $4.04 billion in wages and salaries related to health care in the region. Average payroll for their health care–related operations is $62,945, about 60 percent higher than the average nonfarm wage in the Nashville MSA. Similar to their health care–related employment figures, about 52 percent of the member companies indicated that their health care–related payroll represents less than 30 percent of their annual payroll.

NHCC Members: Office Space and Revenues

NHCC member companies occupy more than 11 million square feet of office space in the Nashville MSA of which 8.4 million are health care–related. This study does not differentiate between the different types of commercial spaces NHCC member companies occupy. The 11 million square feet could be in any combination of retail, office, industrial, or medical office space.[20] As of the second quarter of 2009, office and industrial space in the Nashville MSA is estimated at around 189 million square feet.[21] NHCC member companies occupy about 6 percent of office and industrial space in the Nashville MSA.

Total Nashville-based sales of NHCC member companies are estimated at $37.8 billion, more than double the reported amount of $17 billion in 2005. Total global revenues of these member companies are estimated at around $131 billion. Nearly half of the companies reported annual revenue of less than $10 million. Seventy-nine percent of Nashville revenues come from a group of ten companies. These companies report annual gross revenues of over $1.1 billion dollars each and together make up 94 percent of global revenues for all NHCC member companies. Only 20 companies reported global revenues less than $10 million.

Nashville-based health care–related revenues of NHCC member companies are estimated at $27.6 billion. Globally, their health care–related revenues are $106.9 billion. For 35 percent of reporting companies, health care–related revenues account for less than 30 percent of their total revenues. As part of the survey, BERC also included a question regarding the level of federal research and development grants for scientific and clinical purposes. A total of 54 companies reported $551.4 million in federal research and development, an increase of 107 percent from 2005.

NHCC Members: CEO Confidence Survey

BERC surveyed 149 NHCC member companies regarding their perspective on past, current, and future economic conditions in general and national and local health care in particular. A total of 70 CEOs from member companies responded to this section of the survey for a response rate of 47 percent. The survey took place been November 10, 2009, and January 10, 2010.

Compared to a year ago, current economic conditions in general (2009 compared to 2008).

According to member CEOs, the Nashville MSA is doing much better than the nation. Current economic conditions are better for Nashville for 33 percent of CEOs versus 29 percent for the nation. Nearly half of the CEOs thought current economic conditions for the nation are worse than a year ago, compared to 36 percent indicating the same for Nashville.

Expectations for overall economic conditions for the next year (2010)

NHCC member CEOs are more hopeful about the Nashville MSA economy than about the U.S. economy. Nearly 75 percent of the CEOs expect the Nashville area economy to be better next year while 72 percent of the CEOs expect the U.S. economy to be better. Seven percent of member CEOs expect the U.S. economy to be worse in 12 months compared to 5 percent in the Nashville economy.

Compared to a year ago, current conditions for health care industry and their own companies (2009 compared to 2008)

NHCC member CEOs see their companies better positioned than the national and local health care industry in general. Forty-eight percent of member CEOs see better conditions in their companies compared to a year ago. In comparison, 21 percent of CEOs thought the current U.S. health care industry conditions were better than a year ago. Likewise, 20 percent of CEOs thought the current Nashville health care industry conditions were better than a year ago. Over 40 percent of member CEOs felt the current U.S. health care industry conditions had moderately or substantially gotten worse. Whereas, only 22 percent of CEOs thought the conditions had gotten worse in the Nashville economy and in their companies.

Future Expectations for the Health Care Industry

CEOs are more upbeat about the health care industry in the Nashville MSA than in the nation. Fifty-one percent of member CEOs expect the Nashville health care industry to be substantially or moderately better in 1 year; only 46 percent of CEOs thought this for the U.S. Thirty-four percent expected the health care industry in the U.S. and Nashville would stay the same in the next year.

CEO Confidence Index

The CEO Confidence Index is the average value of standardized scores for the three survey questions highlighted above. These are (1) current general economic conditions compared to a year ago, (2) future expectations for the overall economy, and (3) future expectations for the health care industry.

Overall, the CEO outlook is positive for both the U.S. and Nashville MSA economies. An index value ranges from 0 to 100; a value of 50 and higher suggests a positive outlook. These figures are comparable to the CEO business confidence survey conducted quarterly by the Conference Board. To give a context of the BERC's CEO Confidence Index, the first quarter reading of the Conference Board CEO Confidence Index is 62, suggesting a positive outlook. The health care CEO outlook for the Nashville MSA is 59 while the U.S. outlook is 55.

Hiring and Profit Expectations

The extensive analysis of the health care sector suggests that the industry is a growth industry even in the face of the worst economic recession in recent history. Will this growth trend hold? NHCC member CEOs suggest that this trend will continue. The health care diffusion index, which ranges from −100 being very negative and +100 being very positive, shows a strong hiring expectation in the year following November 2009. The index number is constructed as the difference between the percent of CEOs expecting an increase in hiring and the percent of CEOs expecting a decrease. The current reading of the employment activity is 61 and profits 68. The health care diffusion index is comparable to the business outlook survey for the manufacturing industry by the Federal Reserve Bank of Philadelphia. The April 2010 reading of the Federal Reserve Bank survey is 44 suggesting expanding economic activities in the manufacturing sector.

What is the driving force for increasing profit expectations?

More than two-thirds of the health care CEOs expect the growth in demand for health services to be the driving force for profits. About one-fifth of the health care CEOs cite cost reduction as a primary reason for increasing profit expectations. A mere 4 percent of member CEOs expect price increases or new technology to be the reason of increasing profits.

What is the biggest business concern over the next year?

Before proceeding further, a cautionary note is in order. This survey was conducted between November 10, 2009, and January 10, 2010. A national-level debate on health care reform was heightened during this period. It is not surprising to see nearly three-fifths of the member CEOs citing health care reform as the biggest business concern. It is not clear, however, whether the content of the reform, uncertainty surrounding the reform, or both are the cause of business concerns. Access to capital ranked second with nearly one-fourth of the CEOs citing it as their biggest business concern. Other concerns, accounting for 18 percent of member CEO viewpoints, are listed in order of popularity: increased uninsured patient population, cost of IT, labor unions, and availability of health care professionals.

What are the plans for next year?

Nearly 50 percent of member CEOs indicated that their organizations will grow organically. Mergers and acquisitions are also in the spotlight: 28 percent of CEOs expect their organizations to acquire. Nearly 27 percent indicated that their organizations will focus on operations.

What are the profitable investment areas in the health care business?

Nearly half of NHCC member CEOs suggested that the most profitable sector in the health care business is health care IT. Overall, health care services were cited next by 27 percent, followed by pharmaceuticals/bio-tech industry, 19 percent. Managed care and long-term care were also believed to be profitable forms of investment with 5 percent and 2 percent, respectively.

How important is Nashville to your business?

Does Nashville make a difference for your business? Overall, 95 percent of the NHCC member CEOs indicated that Nashville is important for their business; 53 percent said it is very important.

NOTES

1. According to the 2009 American Hospital Association survey, the number of investor-owned hospitals is around 958. The number of health care companies is extracted from ReferenceUSA and LexisNexis Academic Universe. BERC included

only headquarter companies with over 100 employees and $500,000 annual revenues in these estimates. These companies are part of the broadly defined Nashville health care industry cluster.

2. This section uses the broader "health care and social services" for the Nashville MSA to allow comparison across geographical units. A detailed breakdown of health care services is not publicly available at the Nashville MSA level due to state disclosure rules.

3. State projections are not available for 2008 to 2018.

4. Robert A. Chase, Economic Contribution of the Healthcare Industry to the City of Seattle (Kirkland, WA: Huckell/Weinman Associates, 2004).

5. Market Street Services, Inc. Target Business Analysis: Nashville, TN (Atlanta: Market Street Services, Inc., 2005).

6. Paul Coomes and Raj Narang, Louisville's Health-Related Economy: Size, Character, and Growth (Louisville: University of Louisville, 2001).

7. Many economic impact analyses use the concept of "net new" to describe the economic impact of a project or institution. In this study, BERC has not adjusted employment figures to reflect the local provision of services. The reasons are twofold: (1) a recent patient-origin survey from the Tennessee Department of Health indicates that more than 83 percent of patient days represent patients from outside the Nashville MSA, and (2) the BERC treated at least 10 percent of Nashville-based patient days as recapture given the fact that the Nashville MSA has some of the finest hospitals in the U.S.

8. This report uses a variety of data sources to get an accurate picture of the health care industry within a given context. Because of data suppression issues, certain data components, such as health care industry by segment, are estimated from different sources. This practice then may result in discrepancy in estimating growth rates across the subsectors in this report.

9. NAICS (North American Industrial Classification System) 62 provides an aggregate view of health and social services. Social services includes community services, individual and family services, and child day services. For more information, see www.census.gov/eos/www/naics/.

10. According to a quarterly MarketView report for Nashville by CB Richard Ellis, Nashville had approximately 189 million square feet of office and industrial space in the first quarter of 2009. For details, see www.cbre.com.

11. For a review of literature on locational patterns of company headquarters, see Thomas Klier and William Testa, "Location Trends of Large Company Headquarters During the 1990s" Economic Perspectives (Chicago: Federal Reserve Bank of Chicago, 2002). For detailed information on the concept of cluster and competitive advantage, see Michael Porter, "Location, Competition, and Economic Development: Local Clusters in the Global Economy" Economic Development Quarterly 14 (2000): 15–34.

12. Source: 2008 American Hospital Association Annual Survey Database, ReferenceUSA, LexisNexis Academic Universe, Becker's Hospital Review, and company Web sites.

13. These companies are HCA, Community Health Systems, Vanguard Health Systems, IASIS Healthcare, Ardent Health Services, Capella Healthcare, and LifePoint Hospitals.

14. Notes: Companies with greater than $500,000 in annual revenue and 100 employees are used in this ranking. List includes health care industry cluster companies defined throughout this study. Two sources are used for this profile: LexisNexis Academic Universe and ReferenceUSA.com. Composite score includes relative rankings of each MSA with regard to (1) the number of headquarter companies, (2) their total revenues, and (3) their total number of employees.

15. Average wage represents the average wage for health care practitioners and support occupations.

16. Data reflect the venture capital flow in the following sectors: (1) medical devices and equipment, (2) health services, and (3) biotechnology. Ranking is based on the cumulative value from 1998 to 2009.

17. For a review of literature on different aspects of city rankings, see Fred Cartensen et al., The Second MetroHartford Regional Performance Benchmark (Storrs; Connecticut Center for Economic Analysis: University of Connecticut, 2001).

18. These rankings are based on 56 comparable MSAs in the U.S.

19. For a list of rankings, see the Nashville Area Chamber of Commerce.

20. For a review of the Nashville office market, see quarterly reports at www.colliers.com/Markets/ Nashville and www.cbre.com/USA/Research/Market+Reports/Local+Reports+Worldwide/globalresearch.htm.

21. See CB Richard Ellis MarketView reports for Nashville at www.cbre.com/USA/Research/Market+Reports/Local+Reports+Worldwide/globalresearch.htm.

Chapter 4

Higher Education Institutions in Middle Tennessee

An In-Depth Analysis of Their Impact on the Region from a Comparative Perspective

ECONOMIC GROWTH, KNOWLEDGE, AND UNIVERSITIES: AN INTRODUCTION

Overview

Middle Tennessee is home to 20 major universities with an annual enrollment of nearly 100,000 students. The region includes 41 Tennessee counties, including Davidson, where capital city Nashville is located; Williamson, one of the wealthiest counties in the U.S., and Rutherford, one of the fastest-growing counties in the U.S. Although the Middle Tennessee region includes such vibrant counties, its makeup is quite similar to Tennessee counties overall in terms of per capita income and rural–urban county designations.

What role do these universities play in Middle Tennessee? The primary goal of this study, prepared by the BERC, of the Jennings A. Jones College of Business, at Middle Tennessee State University, for the Presidents' Summit in Middle Tennessee,[1] is to address this broad question. To this end, this endeavor draws insights from many theoretical and empirical studies dealing with such broader topics as economic growth, the knowledge economy, and regional economic competitiveness. We must emphasize at the outset that this study is neither just an economic impact study nor a cost-benefit analysis for public funding purposes. Universities are multifaceted institutions, and the value of their output is often hard to quantify. Therefore, any economic impact figure associated with a group of universities at a regional level represents the least of their many contributions to the health of the regional economy.

BERC designed a comprehensive survey of higher education institutions in Middle Tennessee including a comprehensive set of questions regarding these institutions' spending patterns, students, employment, and other operational and qualitative information, as well as several questions regarding these institutions' interaction with the broader regional environment. In designing the survey, BERC took into account several notable surveys, such as, the Association of University Technology Managers survey and British Higher Education–Business and Community Interaction survey. The detailed survey questions help us understand the broader dynamics in the university–community interactions in Middle Tennessee.

Given the multifaceted nature of these institutions, this study analyzes the broader role of universities in their economic environment. As highlighted by the research on regional economic dynamics, universities are increasingly placed (directly or indirectly) at the center of a regional economy from which economic and social benefits radiate outward. At the center of the debate is the source of economic growth and regional competitiveness, a complex process that generally involves the interaction of several factors including investment in physical and human capital, technological advances, and institutional and policy changes that improve the efficiency of economic organization. In this section, we briefly review some of the key concepts and then explore their relationships with the universities.

Economic Growth

The fundamental issue in macroeconomic theory since Adam Smith has been to explain the sources of the variations in economic growth (fortune) across countries. Adam Smith's *Wealth of Nations* (1776) epitomized the basic precepts of modern macroeconomic theory. Since then, however, the nature of factors that generate nations' wealth has changed considerably. For example, natural endowment is transformed into capital stock and population into human capital. Furthermore, especially since the early 1990s, the process by which economic growth occurs has been redefined to allow the impact of endogenously determined technological progress. A review of economic growth literature indicates that emphasis on technology, knowledge, or human capital in the economic development process is not new. What is new, however, is the understanding of economic growth dynamics, which have changed long-held views on the limits of economic growth (diminishing versus increasing returns). In light of this new understanding, economic growth is defined as a function of growth in capital stock, labor force, and technological progress (Armstrong and Taylor, 2000).

At the micro level, sources of economic growth and regional competitiveness are closely tied to the productivity of a region's workforce. The most prominent of this line of work is Michael Porter's *The Competitive Advantage of Nations* (1990), which treats labor productivity as the single most important factor differentiating one country from another. Labor productivity, in turn, is determined by the capital-labor ratio, endogenous technical progress, and human capital (Armstrong and Taylor, 2000).

In his empirical investigation of the sources of economic prosperity, Richard Florida (2005), further advances the notion of human capital and technology as driving forces for regional prosperity. Florida (2005), argues that economic prosperity is a function of three T's: talent, technology, and tolerance. The last of these, tolerance, as a source of economic growth ties economic growth and regional competitiveness to another strand of theoretical approach related to the quality of civic life or human capital: social capital.

The social capital literature has gained interdisciplinary prominence after such seminal works as Coleman (1990), Putnam (1993), and OECD (2001). Although some economists disagree on whether social capital could be treated the same as human capital, many, nevertheless, acknowledge that social capital enhances human capital. In an extensive treatment of the issue, Westlund (2006) argues that social capital can be treated as a type of knowledge that enhances the level of human capital (p. 41).

Knowledge

It appears that knowledge, either in the form of human capital or technological advancement, has become the common denominator in much economic growth and regional competitiveness literature. Prominent treatment of the issue can be found in literature on human capital (Romer, 1986), labor productivity and knowledge (Porter, 1990), talent and technology (Florida, 2005), and science and technology (Kozmetsky et al., 2004). At the forefront of economic development literature, knowledge—its creation, dissemination, and transfer—is considered an important part of wealth creation (Wignaraja, 2003, p. 4; Westlund, 2006, p. 11).

Making knowledge a source of wealth creation has important implications for the role of universities and communities. Garmise (2005) emphasizes two critical components of knowledge: investment in knowledge production and human capital. These investments are inherent in the production function of modern universities. Furthermore, not only these investments, but also, other characteristics of knowledge societies such as tolerance (Florida, 2005) and social capital (Putnam, 1993) are critically linked to the presence of knowledge institutions in a community.

Universities

A summary treatment of economic growth literature indicates that the quality of many factors of production depends on investment in knowledge production and human capital. The role of universities in the U.S. increased dramatically after the Bayh-Dole Act of 1980. This increasing role also coincides with the development of theories on the role of human capital and knowledge in economic prosperity. The title of Kozmetsky et al.'s (2004) book, *New Wealth: Commercialization of Science and Technology for Business and Economic Development*, aptly describes community and university interactions in the knowledge economy.

Universities' role in their communities is not, however, limited to technological development and human capital creation: they play a critical leadership role in transforming the economic landscape of their communities.[2] In many communities, universities are often the largest employers transforming the urban landscape through their employment, spending, and land purchases (Perry and Wiewel, 2005).

The literature on modern universities shows a diverse set of missions and organizational goals that differently affect their surrounding regions, ranging from the traditional functions of teaching and public service to the recent activities of licensing inventions and engaging collaboratively in research with private sector industries (Glasson, 2003; Thanki, 1999). Goldstein, Maier, and Luger (1995) indicate eight university functions leading to economic development impact: (a) knowledge creation, (b) human capital creation, (c) transfer of existing know-how, (d) technological innovation, (e) capital investment, (f) regional leadership, (g) influence on regional milieu, and (h) knowledge infrastructure production.

Figure 4.1 describes the multifaceted role universities play in their communities. Three major categories described in Figure 4.1—knowledge institutions, a skilled labor force, and strategic partnerships with the community—also represent three foundations of a knowledge economy. In general, there are two major strands in the literature on the growth of a regional economy: one focusing on higher education institutions' effects on regional economies, also called backward linkages or inputs, the other on the contribution of human capital and technological advancements to regional economies. However, the often-understated aspect of the university-community relationship is their strategic partnership.

Economic Impact of Universities

Measurable economic impacts of universities may involve either the impact of universities as operating institutions and their related activities or the impact of an additional year of schooling on economic growth. Over the years, a substantial number of studies have emerged dealing with the former issue. A sample of reviewed studies regarding the economic impact of universities is provided in the reference section. A study that treats the role of these institutions somewhat differently is Goldstein and Drucker (2006), which examines the influences of four-year colleges and universities in the U.S. at the metropolitan level focusing on the internal and external factors that affect

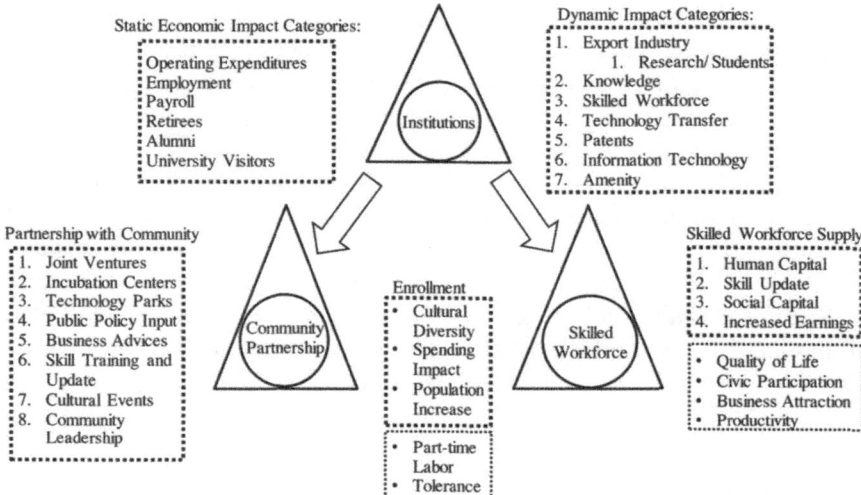

Figure 4.1 The Knowledge Economy and Higher Education Institutions: Institutions, Skilled Workforce, and Strategic Partnership. *Source*: Figure created by author

the generation of regional economic development impacts. They found that knowledge-based university activities, such as teaching and basic research, have a substantial impact on regional earnings gains. Furthermore, the impacts are higher in small- and medium-sized regions than in large regions.

Similar to the economic impact assessment, many studies deal with the return to higher education and the contribution of an additional year of schooling to economic growth.[3] Human capital accumulation may allow people to better obtain and use the technologies already existing worldwide or better produce new, previously nonexistent technologies. Mankiw et al. (1992) use school enrollment rates as a human capital investment proxy for human capital stocks in cross-county growth regressions to examine whether the Solow growth model is consistent with the international variation in the standard of living. It shows an augmented Solow model that includes accumulation of human as well as physical capital provides an excellent description of the cross-country data. Benhabib and Spiegel (1994) use a cross-country sample and find that human capital is more important in technology adoption (balanced growth path effect) than in technology development (balanced growth rate effect).

Groot and Oosterbeek (1994) show that not all years of education are rewarded at the same rate. A review of studies for the U.S. shows that the rate of return for vocational qualifications is 5 to 10 percent higher than for general qualifications.

Yong, Levy, and Higgins (2004) use county-level data to investigate the roles of different types of human capital accumulation in U.S. growth determination. Their findings suggest that the percent of the population with an advanced degree (college and above) is positively correlated with growth.

Some analyses of the economic effects of education have focused on an assessment of the rate of return. A comparison of the incomes of the educated with those of the uneducated allows education's rate of return to be calculated. Christopher and Martin (1994) argue that education raises the effective size of the labor force because it increases the labor productivity of individuals. During a period in which the education standard of the population is rising, this stock adjustment effect will lead to economic growth. Lucas (1988) indicates that knowledge does not completely disappear with the death of an educated generation but that some of it is inherited by its successors. Then high levels of education will be associated with rapid rates of technical progress.

Study Goals

The goal of this study is to provide a comprehensive assessment of the role of higher education institutions in Middle Tennessee. To this end, this study:

1. Estimates the economic impact of higher education institutions on the regional economy
2. Compares skilled labor supply and demand conditions in Middle Tennessee
3. Provides an analysis of university–community interactions and
4. Compares the Middle Tennessee region with peer areas utilizing publicly available higher education indicators.

General Methodology

As the summary conceptual framework in Figure 4.2 illustrates, this study highlights both static and dynamic impacts of universities and how they lead to the societal impact. Static impacts include expenditures from operating, visitors, and students; employment; population; and retirees. Research and innovation, occupational supply and training, and amenities fall under the category of dynamic impact. The static and dynamic impacts together contribute to societal impacts. While some of these impacts are easier to quantify than others, they include: economic growth, fiscal stability, cultural diversity, business attraction and retention, and regional competitiveness.

Data

This study relies on data from the BERC's survey, IPEDS (Integrated Postsecondary Education Data System) database, and several governmental and institutional websites. First, BERC surveyed 20 higher education institutions in Middle Tennessee. BERC received completed surveys from 15 institutions (75 percent response rate). For the remaining five institutions, BERC utilized the IPEDS and the websites of individual institutions. The following 20 institutions are profiled in this study in alphabetical order:

> American Baptist College, Aquinas College, Austin Peay State University, Belmont University, Columbia State Community College, Cumberland University, Fisk University, Free Will Baptist College, Lipscomb University, Martin Methodist College, Meharry Medical College, Middle Tennessee State University, Motlow State Community College, Nashville State Technical Community College, Tennessee State University, Tennessee Technological University, Trevecca Nazarene University, University of the South, Vanderbilt University, and Volunteer State Community College.

Additionally, BERC consulted the following data sources to construct regional profiles:

1. U.S. Census Bureau (www.census.gov)
2. Bureau of Labor Statistics (www.bls.gov)
3. Tennessee Department of Labor and Workforce Development (http://tennessee.gov/labor-wfd)
4. Tennessee Department of Health (www.state.tn.us/health/)
5. Bureau of Economic Analysis (www.bea.gov)
6. U.S. Department of Education (www.ed.gov) and
7. websites of individual higher education institutions across the selected MSAs.

Study Region and MSAs

The study region in this study is defined as 41 Middle Tennessee counties. The selection of MSAs for comparison was guided by the Nashville Area Chamber of Commerce. These MSAs are Columbus, OH; Indianapolis, IN; Atlanta, GA; Raleigh-Cary, NC; Charlotte, NC; Jacksonville, FL; Dallas, TX; Kansas City, MO; Louisville, KY; Birmingham, AL; Denver, CO; and Richmond, VA. In comparing the Middle Tennessee region to these selected MSAs, we must emphasize that we did not attempt to define similar regions for the MSAs involved in this study.

Universities in the Selected MSAs

In selecting universities in other MSAs, we used the following criteria: all private, nonprofit universities, public universities, and community colleges are included in the analysis. The total number of higher education institutions involved in this study was about 240 across all regions including Middle Tennessee.

The rest of the report is structured as follows: first, we provide an economic impact analysis of higher education institutions in Middle Tennessee; second, we look at skilled labor supply and demand conditions in Middle Tennessee; third, we address higher education's relationship with the business community; and last, we provide a comparative perspective on higher education institutions in Middle Tennessee and conclude the report.

ECONOMIC IMPACT OF HIGHER EDUCATION INSTITUTIONS IN MIDDLE TENNESSEE: INPUT-OUTPUT ANALYSIS

Overview

Universities benefit many segments of a community from individuals through higher earnings, to governments through a stable tax revenue base, to the community itself through creating a competitive business environment and enhancing civic participation. Many of these benefits are difficult to quantify. Universities, however, also have a function similar to many businesses in a community: they purchase goods and services from local vendors, they employ people, and they host events and conferences attracting people from other areas to the region. These functions of universities alone may have a significant economic impact on a region.

Considering the fact that some universities are the largest employers in their communities, their impact on their community amounts to a sizable figure. We must acknowledge, however, that the traditional economic impact of universities is only one of their many contributions to their communities as highlighted in the first chapter.

This chapter solely deals with the traditional economic impact of universities on their communities. First, we provide an overview of economic impact studies, study assumptions, and methodology. Second, we examine major economic impact categories and underlying assumptions for each category using the survey results. Finally, we provide the results of the economic impact analysis.

An Overview of Economic Impact Studies

The role a university plays in its community is widely acknowledged. In the past two decades, a significant number of economic impact studies emerged, many of which address the economic impact of a single university on its community. A selected list of reviewed studies for this report is provided in the reference section. Methodologically, many of these studies utilize minimum data on capital expenditure, operating expenditure, student expenditure, and payroll. Furthermore, economic impact studies often utilize one of the following three economic impact programs: Regional Economic Impact Modeling, Inc. (REMI at www.remi.com); IMpact Analysis for PLANning (IMPLAN at www.implan.com); and the Bureau of Economic Analysis' regional multipliers (RIMS II at www.bea.gov).

Although many university economic impact studies deal with a single university or university system's economic impact, in recent years, there is a resurgence of interest at the regional level to engage universities in economic development or revitalization efforts. In these efforts, the role of universities in the success of Silicon Valley or Route 128 plays an important role.[4] A notable recent example of a multi-university economic impact study is *Engines of Economic Growth: The Economic Impact of Boston's Eight Research Universities.* Similarly, this study looks at the economic impact of 20 Middle Tennessee higher education institutions in 41 counties.

A university's impact on its community is significant due to both backward and forward linkages. Backward linkages (also called inputs or static) are usually easy to quantify by examining university spending on goods and services, employee spending, student spending, and visitor spending. Forward linkages (also called outputs or dynamic impacts) are actually more important than backward linkages; however, they are not easily quantifiable. One forward linkage is the impact a university's research has on labor productivity or the university's production of a skilled labor force supply. Additionally, universities improve their regions' quality of life through diversity, preservation, and cultural activities as well as supplying much-needed public policy input on a variety of regional issues.

Given the difficulty of capturing all dynamic impacts of a university on a community, many studies attempt to capture the economic impact of backward linkages while acknowledging the broader community impacts of the universities. Similarly, this chapter deals with the impact of 20 universities on Middle Tennessee through backward linkages, and we treat some of the forward linkages in the next chapters.

Study Assumptions

As mentioned previously, this chapter deals with the impact of backward linkages examining capital expenditures, noncapital operating expenditures, student expenditures, visitor expenditures, and payroll. Every economic analysis relies on several general assumptions or guiding principles regarding the economic activity under investigation. In measuring economic impact, we make several assumptions and adjustments as follows:

1. *The region.* A meaningful regional boundary is critical to any economic impact study. Since we are dealing with 20 universities spread across Middle Tennessee, we constructed a regional model that involves 41 Middle Tennessee counties.
2. *Substitution effect.* We assume that 20 universities represent the entire universe of higher education in the study region. In other words, if these universities were closed down, the region would lose all student population. Therefore, total enrollment in these 20 universities is treated as "net new" to the region.
3. *Counterfactual approach.* Many universities in the region have a history of more than a century. Since they are already in the baseline economy, in order to measure the impact of their operations, we need to remove them from the baseline economy. The difference between the baseline economy and the new equilibrium level after the removal of university operation and related activities represents the total economic impact.
4. *Physical buildings remain intact.* In measuring economic impact, we are dealing only with the current operation of these universities and related activities. The assumption is that if a university were closed down, like any business, all activities would cease to operate. We are not, however, tearing down the physical buildings; they remain intact.
5. *Local versus out of region.* All capital and noncapital expenditures are adjusted using the university-supplied survey data. Only expenditures made in Middle Tennessee were included in the analysis.
6. *Residency adjustment.* Similar to the expenditure data, only university employees residing in Middle Tennessee and their payrolls were included in the analysis.
7. *Visitor expenditures.* The number of university visitors was estimated from a variety of sources including survey data. University visitors from outside Middle Tennessee were included in the final calculations of visitor expenditures. A certain number of assumptions were developed to calculate a minimum number of university visitor days. Visitors' spending pattern is estimated from surveys conducted for non-university-related events in Tennessee.

Methodology

Concept of Economic Impact

University-related spending initiates a round-by-round sequence of impacts on local business revenue, value added, wages, and employment. University spending for goods and services, for example, increases sales by companies that provide these goods and services. These companies purchase inputs including labor, machinery, and supplies and materials in order to produce output. The effect of the initial expenditure eventually works its way through the local economy.

The round-by-round increases in economic activity that characterize the multiplier process become smaller with every round due to leakages from the spending stream. Leakages consist of spending for goods or services not produced in the local economy. For example, university spending for personal computers from a manufacturer in North Carolina generates no economic impact for the Middle Tennessee economy aside from the provision of delivery services.

Economists use multipliers to estimate the sum of the round-by-round effects of expenditures. Typically, multipliers estimate three effects: direct, indirect, and induced. The direct effect consists of the initial change in expenditures. The indirect effect is the sum of the round-by-round increases in business spending for inputs, not including labor. The induced effect is the sum of the round-by-round increases in employee spending due to increased payrolls and household incomes.[5]

Economic Impact Model and Modeling Approach

Many economists use IMPLAN (Impact Analysis for Planning) software to help estimate multipliers for local economies. The IMPLAN software package was originally developed by the U.S. Forest Service and is now maintained and sold by a private research company. Our model estimates 20 universities' impact on the 41-county Middle Tennessee region by examining the effects if the 20 universities were to close down.

Conceptual Framework

The basic framework of this study is built around a conceptual model that treats 20 universities as an economic entity nested in the Middle Tennessee economy. Economic impact radiates from these universities across the 41-county region. Figure 4.2 identifies the economic impact categories of 20 universities considered by this study that have both direct and indirect effects upon the regional economy.

In this chapter, we seek to quantify five major impact categories as presented in Figure 4.2: capital expenditures, noncapital operating expenditures, student expenditure, visitor expenditure, and employee spending. In the following sections, a detailed explanation of expenditure estimates is provided.

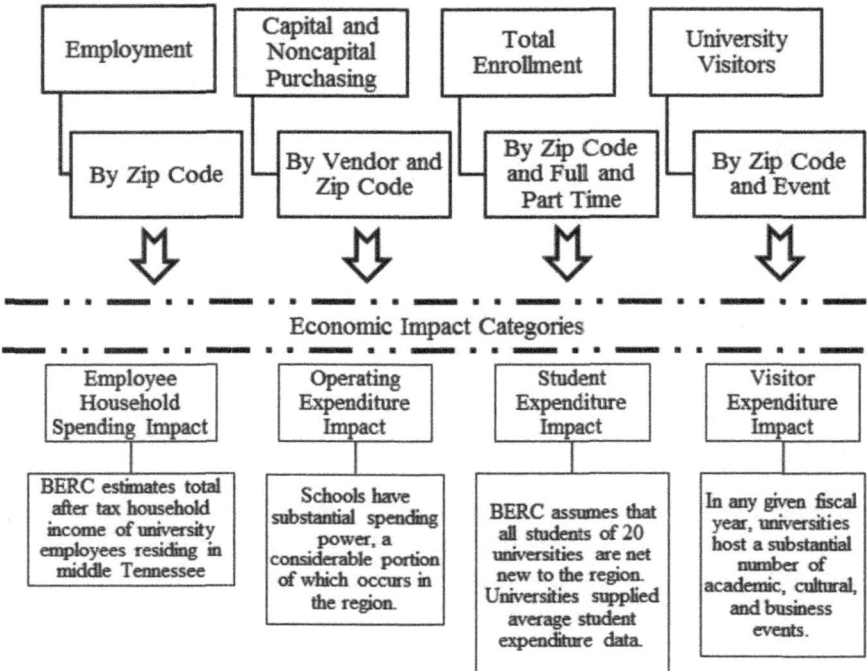

Figure 4.2 Data Categories for Economic Impact. *Source*: Figure created by author

Economic Impact Categories, Assumptions, and Impact Results

For each of five economic impact categories as well as a separate Vanderbilt Hospital economic impact, we first provide assumptions regarding the underlying data and then present the detailed economic impact results.

Capital Expenditures (Assumptions and Estimates)

Based on the BERC survey and IPEDS data for non-reporting institutions, in FY 2004–2005, 20 universities in Middle Tennessee spent an estimated $303 million on capital projects. This figure does not include capital expenditures associated with Vanderbilt Hospital. Of this amount, an estimated $249 million was spent in Middle Tennessee. Of all expenditures made in Middle Tennessee, 75 percent, or $187 million, were in construction. Other equipments made up the majority of out-of-area spending with 60 percent of $54 million.

In examining the impact of capital expenditures, we take into account the expense of building and maintaining university facilities as well as equipment costs. The capital expenditures are then distributed among the appropriate IMPLAN sectors constructed for the Middle Tennessee region.

Economic Impact of Capital Expenditures

Universities in Middle Tennessee directly injected $249 million into Middle Tennessee in construction and equipment-related expenditures. Taking into account indirect and induced impacts, the capital expenditures of the 20 universities generated a total of:

1. $457 million in business revenue
2. $183 million in personal income
3. 4,722 jobs and
4. $13.6 million in state and local taxes.

Of the 4,722 jobs attributed to universities' capital expenditures, more than half (52 percent) were in construction, followed by 10 percent in retail and 9 percent in manufacturing. When we examine the distribution of business revenue resulting from universities' capital expenditures, we find that of $457 million in business revenue, 44 percent is in construction, 16 percent in manufacturing, and 6 percent in retail trade.

Noncapital Operating Expenditures (Assumptions and Estimates)

In addition to capital expenditures, Middle Tennessee universities impact the region through noncapital operating expenditures. Not taking into account the contributions of Vanderbilt University Hospital (which will be treated separately), payroll and total noncapital operating expenditures in the Middle Tennessee region amount to $748.456 million. Total noncapital operating expenditure of 20 universities was estimated at $1.088 billion in 2005, of which 69 percent ($748 million) remained in Middle Tennessee. Within in the region, these expenditures primarily consisted of grants and subsidies ($99 million), other supplies ($90 million), and consulting services ($81). Major expenditures made outside the region included consulting services, $44 million, and travel expenditures, $39 million. These estimates are primarily based on the survey responses of 75 percent of 20 universities in Middle Tennessee.

Economic Impact of Noncapital Operating Expenditures

The spending of 20 universities on goods and services in Middle Tennessee was substantial in 2005. The estimated total impact of noncapital operating expenditures of 20 universities was as follows:

1. $1.254 billion in business revenue
2. $446 million in personal income

3. 10,452 jobs (excluding employees of 20 institutions) and
4. $42 million in state and local taxes.

Which sectors of the regional economy benefit most from noncapital operating expenditures of the 20 universities? The largest business revenue impact took place in manufacturing (13 percent), professional-scientific and technical services (12 percent), and finance and insurance (11 percent). In terms of distribution of employment impact of 10,452 jobs, educational services accounted for the largest share (16 percent) followed by professional-scientific and technical services (14 percent).

Employee Household Expenditures (Assumptions and Estimates)

In this section, we do not include the wages, salaries, and employment figures from Vanderbilt University Hospital, which will be treated separately. Universities in Middle Tennessee employ 29,422 people in the region including part-time employees and student workers. Of 29,422 employees, only two percent live outside the study region.

According to survey data, employees in Middle Tennessee earned an estimated $988 million in 2005: nearly $13 million paid to student workers and graduate assistants, and $20 million earned by employees residing outside Middle Tennessee. Total adjusted payroll for faculty and staff is estimated at $955.603 million before taxes.

Economic Impact

The economic impact of the 20 universities' payroll is significant. After taking into account federal taxes and other deductions, the payroll impact of the 20 universities is estimated at:

1. $1.34 billion in business revenue
2. $443 million in personal income (in addition to initial earnings of university employees)
3. 33,556 jobs (including 21,487 Full-time equivalent of 20 universities) and
4. $74 million in state and local taxes.

How are business revenue and employment impacts distributed across the major sectors? The largest business payroll revenue impact occurred in health and social services (13 percent), manufacturing (11 percent), finance and insurance (11 percent), and retail trade (10 percent). In terms of jobs, due to the ownership mix of universities (public and private, not-for-profit), the two largest sectors are educational services (40 percent) and government (26 percent).

Visitor Expenditures (Assumptions and Estimates)

In addition to employee expenditures, visitors to Middle Tennessee universities create a significant economic impact. Not including visitors to Vanderbilt University Hospital, the total number of net new visitors to Middle Tennessee universities is estimated at 307,795 day-trippers and 116,938 overnight visitors. Those visitors staying overnight accounted for an estimated 264,092 hotel nights in Middle Tennessee.

University visitors in Middle Tennessee spent an estimated $50 million on goods and services: nearly $14 million spent by day-trippers and $36 million by those visitors staying overnight in the region.[6] We must, however, emphasize that visitor estimates and their total spending reflect conservative figures.

Economic Impact of University Visitors

Even though estimates are conservative, university visitors have a significant impact on the regional economy. The findings suggest that universities are major visitor centers, attracting people with diverse backgrounds from all over the world. As stated above, there are many venues through which the 20 universities attract people to the region. The diversity of venues signifies the contribution of the 20 universities to social and cultural as well as academic life in Middle Tennessee.

In terms of university visitors' contribution to the regional economy, visitors' spending generates:

1. $72 million in business revenue
2. $22 million in personal income
3. 858 jobs and
4. $5 million in state and local taxes.

Table 4.1 Visitor Assumptions and Total Number of Day-trippers and Hotel Nights (20 Universities)

	Attendance/ Events	Day-trippers	Overnight Stays	Hotel Nights
Families of Freshmen	14,267	6,661	7,606	11,300
Youth Camp Attendance	10,216	10,216	0	0
Home Games/Events	796	201,000	40,200	80,400
Cultural Events	870	43.500	0	0
Business Events	437	42,826	874	1,748
Conferences	479	3,592	68,258	170,644
Total	n/a	307,795	116,938	264,092

Source: Table created by author

Which sectors of the economy are impacted most by the visitor spending? It is not surprising that 54 percent of the business revenue is in accommodation and food services followed by 12 percent in retail trade. In terms of employment impact, 68 percent of jobs are in accommodation and food services and 14 percent in retail trade.

Student Expenditures (Assumptions and Estimates)

Students represent an important part of this economic impact study of higher education institutions. Apart from their contribution to the regional economy as part-time employees in their respective universities and across businesses, their spending in the regional economy is significant. Based on the BERC survey data, total enrollment including continuing education and online enrollment is estimated at 110,182 in 2005. These students injected more than $1 billion into the regional economy. An estimated 21 percent of students stayed on campus, 57 percent off-campus, and 23 percent with family.

Estimated student expenditures are based on three categories of full-time and part-time students: on-campus, off-campus, and staying with family. Estimated student expenditure profiles are derived from the BERC survey of higher education institutions. Of $1.1 billion in student expenditures, $792 million belongs to students living off campus, $184 million to those living on campus, and $84 million those staying with family. In terms of expenditure categories, housing is the largest with $253 million, followed by food and beverages ($218 million) and transportation related ($156 million).

Economic Impact of Student Expenditures

What is the total economic impact of student expenditures on the Middle Tennessee economy? The total economic impact of student expenditures is estimated at:

Table 4.2 Distribution of Student Expenditure by Type of Accommodation

Expenditure Type	On-Campus	Off-Campus	Stay with Family	Total
Housing	$0	$253,390,060	$0	$253,390,060
Household Operation	$0	$58,304,617	$0	$58,304,617
Other Durables	$0	$29,977,227	$0	$29,977,227
Food and Beverages	$64,202,914	$154,163,260	$0	$218,366,173
Vehicles and Parts	$19,093,945	$51,985,430	$20,922,595	$92,001,970
Transportation	$33,711,675	$87,161,200	$35,079,800	$155,952,675
Clothing	$19,536,040	$37,448,187	$0	$56,984,227
Other Service	$29,345,983	$69,189,391	$27,838,327	$126,373,701
Computer & Furniture	$11,433,500	$31,129,000	$0	$42,562,500
Medical Care	$7,164,993	$19,507,507	$0	$26,672,500
Total	$184,489,050	$792,255,878	$83,840,722	$1,060,585,650

Source: Table created by author

1. $1.5 billion in business revenue
2. $384 million in personal income
3. 10,064 jobs and
4. $79 million in state and local taxes.

Which major sectors of the regional economy benefited most from student spending? The largest business revenue impact occurred in real estate and rental (27 percent), retail trade (18 percent), and transportation and warehousing (16 percent). In terms of employment impact, retail trade (31 percent), real estate and rental (17 percent), and transportation and warehousing (13 percent) were the largest beneficiaries.

Total Higher Education Economic Impact

Middle Tennessee's 20 universities have a significant impact on the regional economy. Taking into account expenditures of the institutions themselves, their employees, visitors, and students, they generate a total of:

1. $4.6 billion in business revenue
2. $1.5 billion in personal income (in addition to $955 million for their own initial payroll)
3. 59,652 jobs and
4. $214 million in state and local tax revenues

Vanderbilt University Hospital

Above and beyond the economic impacts described heretofore, Vanderbilt University Hospital, as a major research hospital, makes its own unique and significant contribution to Middle Tennessee's economy. This study does not provide a comprehensive assessment of Vanderbilt University Hospital's clinical services. Such an assessment would be likely to increase the magnitude of the hospital's economic impact because several unique services keep patients in the region. Furthermore, a substantial amount of charity care is not discussed in this report. That said, Vanderbilt University Hospital's economic impact is nonetheless remarkable.

Vanderbilt University Hospital employed 8,670 people residing in Middle Tennessee at an estimated payroll of $417 million, of which $346 million was disposable income. The hospital's operating expenditures (excluding payroll) totaled more than $500 million, of which 46 percent ($223 million) was spent in the region. Furthermore, Vanderbilt is the largest hospital in terms of inpatient and outpatient days in Tennessee. One million clinical visitors seek treatment at Vanderbilt, of which more than a quarter were from outside the region. These clinical visitors spend a total of 279,383 days at Vanderbilt, 54,149 of which include hotel stays for family members accompanying patients injecting a total of $17.5 million into the region's economy.

Economic Impact of Vanderbilt University Hospital

Based on the assumptions above, Vanderbilt University Hospital's total economic impact was estimated at:

1. $872 million in total business revenue
2. $246 million in personal income (in addition to its own payroll of $346 million)
3. 15,526 jobs in the region and
4. $41 million in state and local taxes.

It is important to emphasize that due to the modeling approach we followed, the initial personal income (payroll) associated with Vanderbilt University Hospital and the 20 universities is not present in the personal income category throughout the earlier portion of this chapter. Therefore, the personal income figures in this chapter should be interpreted as "in addition to these institutions' payroll."

Grand Total

In calculating the total economic impact of the 20 universities and Vanderbilt University Hospital, BERC included the initial payroll of the 20 universities and the hospital in value added (GDP equivalent) and personal income. Therefore, the results should be interpreted as the total economic impact figures inclusive of all university and hospital activities as well as the initial payroll of these institutions. In findings previously discussed, the personal income effect of household expenditures was presented as being in addition to initial payroll of these universities. In 2005, the 20 universities and Vanderbilt University Hospital accounted for:

1. $5.6 billion in business revenue,
    a. For every dollar of direct spending, an additional in $0.53 in business revenue was created through a multiplier effect.
2. $2.9 billion in personal income (including initial payrolls),
    a. For every dollar of personal income paid by the 20 universities, an additional $0.61 of personal income was created in the study area.
3. 75,178 jobs, and
    a. For every 100 jobs directly created by universities, an additional 65 jobs are created across the regional economy.
4. $255 million in state and local taxes were generated.

Conclusion

This chapter of the study analyzed the economic impact of five university-related economic activities as well as Vanderbilt University Hospital. As mentioned frequently throughout this study, the economic impact figures related to these activities represent only a small portion of the broader economic contribution of the 20 universities to the Middle Tennessee economy. However, given the scope of the economic impact of these institutions, it is accurate to portray these institutions as "engines of growth."

HIGHER EDUCATION INSTITUTIONS AND SKILLED LABOR SUPPLY AND DEMAND IN MIDDLE TENNESSEE

Overview

In the knowledge economy, skill is an important source of wealth. As the structure of the economy changes, so does the demand for skilled workforce. Any discussion about the knowledge economy puts the universities and colleges at the center of debate as they are major suppliers of a skilled workforce in a community. The universities and colleges in a community are on both sides of the skilled labor demand and supply equations.

The major sources of a skilled workforce are net in-migration and immigration and local supply through universities and colleges. Net in-migration and immigration includes (1) students and (2) skilled adults. Students come to the region to enroll in local higher education institutions. After graduation, some students choose to stay in the region and become part of the local skilled labor force. There are also skilled adults who are attracted to the region. An important portion of these skilled adults work at the local higher education institutions. In this sense, the local universities and colleges themselves are magnets for the skilled workforce from other regions. Furthermore, the local universities and colleges play major roles for non-university- or college-related skilled workforce as they provide lifelong training opportunities.

The local supply of a skilled workforce takes place through two major channels: high school graduates find educational opportunities in the regional institutions. After graduation, they work at local businesses or setup their own businesses. As for the workforce in the region, universities provide lifelong learning opportunities to update their skill levels. On demand side, some skilled workforce in the region find employment opportunities at the local higher education institutions at various levels of their careers.

While universities and colleges play considerable roles in both sides of labor supply and demand equation in a region, their roles have become critically important because of the changes in the demand for skilled workforce. The nationwide long-term occupational growth projections indicate a growing

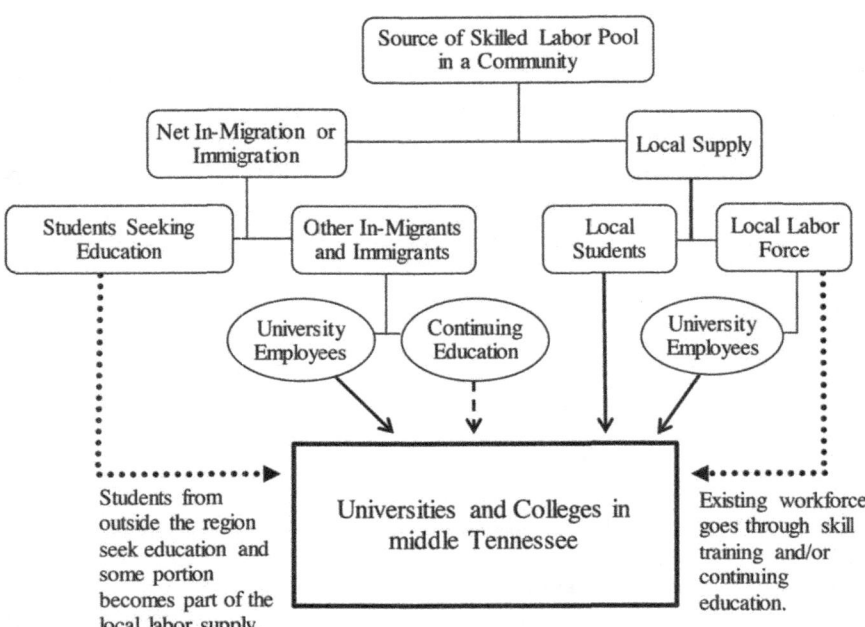

Figure 4.3 Universities are at the Center of the Skilled Labor Pool in Middle Tennessee

demand for college educated workforce. As the large portion of workforce (baby boomers) is expected to retire in the next five to ten years, new replacements for many positions require a different skill-set from the skill-set of retiring workforce. In the U.S., the top 15 "much faster growing" occupations[7] are expected to add nearly 3.7 million jobs, of which 1.8 million are expected to require at least a bachelors' degree. Overall, these 15 occupations represent nearly 6 percent of total occupations profiled but 20 percent of total projected job growths between 2004 and 2014. The projected 1.8 million jobs in the 15 occupations, for which at least a college education is required, alone represent nearly 10 percent of total projected job growth between 2004 and 2014.

What are the supply and demand conditions for the skilled labor in Middle Tennessee? How well do higher education institutions in Middle Tennessee meet the demand for a skilled labor force? A detailed analysis of supply and demand conditions and how well Middle Tennessee's higher education institutions are meeting demand is critically important for both higher education institutions and local businesses. In particular, a substantial supply shortage is expected across all occupations throughout the region as the baby boomer generation approaches retirement age. Furthermore, more and more occupations require additional education, suggesting that estimates based on the 2004 educational attainment levels may be substantially biased toward the lower educational attainment level.

As part of the larger study, this chapter addresses skilled labor force supply and demand conditions in Middle Tennessee. The rest of the chapter is organized as follows: first, we deal with brief methodological issues. Second, we highlight the findings on the supply side of the workforce and look at the supply and demand relationship. Third, we deal with the demand side of the issue and highlight the role higher education plays in meeting the demand for the skilled labor force.

Methodology

BERC utilized several sources of data to analyze supply and demand for a skilled labor force in Middle Tennessee. We must acknowledge, however, that the estimations provided here do not reflect the price accounting for the skilled labor force supply and demand due to the following reasons: first, BERC's estimates of the skilled labor force supply are based on the survey of higher education institutions. Extrapolating to all universities from the limited number of responses includes a certain level of measurement error. Second, the skilled labor supply analysis does not include in-migration and immigration of the skilled labor force to the region. Third, the skilled workforce demand analysis does not include job turnover as a source of demand. Finally, employment by occupation projections is used to estimate the total growth for each occupation. Furthermore, net replacement rates for each occupation are estimated from national employment by occupations projections. Since Tennessee's underlying population dynamics are different from those of the nation, the net replacement rates may be more or less different in Middle Tennessee as opposed to the United States. Similarly, BLS estimates are used to estimate the number of occupations requiring certain educational attainment. BLS calculates this information using Current Population Survey Results. The local employment conditions may not completely overlap with the national conditions.

Data Source

In this analysis, the underlying data is drawn from the following sources:

1. *A BERC survey of higher education institutions.* BERC surveyed 20 major Middle Tennessee universities and colleges. Even though the response rate for specific alumni-related questions was low, we nevertheless received some responses that allowed us to extrapolate the findings to all 20 universities and colleges. BERC specifically asked the following questions to 20 universities and colleges for the purpose of identifying the true scope of skilled labor supply:
   a. *What is the number of alumni living in Middle Tennessee?*
   b. *What is the average number of graduates each year?*

c. *What is the percent of graduates remaining in the region?*
   d. *Please provide number of graduates by occupation.*
2. *Integrated Postsecondary Data System (IPEDS).* When the information about a college is missing, we utilized this deeply rich higher education database to fill the information gap.
3. *The U.S. Bureau of Labor Statistics.* This is the key source of data for a variety of workforce characteristics. We obtained employment projections by replacement as well as occupational employment by educational attainment data from the Bureau of Labor Statistics.
4. *The Tennessee Department of Labor and Workforce Development.* Employment projections by occupations between 2004 and 2014 are constructed from the Tennessee Department of Labor and Workforce Development (TDLWD). We first obtained complete employment projections datasets for individual Local Workforce Investment Area (LWIA); then, we aggregated LWIA projections to get Middle Tennessee projections.
5. *Websites of individual higher education institutions.* BERC staff visited the website of each university and college to get information about their student characteristics, alumni information, university publications dealing with alumni relations, and other information regarding the characteristics of graduates.

Although BERC has made every attempt to capture skilled labor force dynamics as they are related to higher education institutions, BERC's calculations do not reflect precise figures because of low survey response rates. The findings, however, do provide some insights about the skilled labor supply and demand conditions in Middle Tennessee.

Profile of Enrollment and Graduates: Supply Side

According to survey data, 98,931 degree-seeking students are enrolled in 20 Middle Tennessee higher education institutions in 2005. Of this potential skilled labor force, 23 percent are enrolled in Associate's degree programs, 61 percent are pursuing Bachelor's degrees, and 16 percent are enrolled in Master's or Doctoral degree programs.

Based on survey results and extensive review of alumni-related data from 20 universities and colleges' websites, we estimated that nearly 60 percent of the 17,144 new graduates become a part of local skilled workforce. Of the graduates remaining in the region, 23 percent were Associate's degree earners, 61 percent were Bachelor's degree earners, and 16 percent were Master's and Doctorate degree earners.

The calculation of total number of alumni of the 20 universities in Middle Tennessee is based on several assumptions. A few universities supplied us detailed alumni information. In this case, we used the university or college

Table 4.3 Supply of Skilled Workforce in Middle Tennessee

Average Number of Graduates Each Year	17,144
Estimated Percent Remaining in the Region	60%
Number of Graduates Remaining in the Region	10,286
Estimated Distribution of Graduates Remaining in the Region by Degree Type	
Associate's Degree	2,408
Bachelor's Degree	6,257
Master's Degree	1,409
Doctorate	212
Total	10,286

Source: Table created by author

supplied alumni data. For some universities and colleges, we obtained alumni information through alumni newsletters and websites of their university foundations and alumni relations. For the remaining universities and colleges, the BERC used the following assumptions:

1. Average number of students graduating in the last three to five years depending on data availability
2. Average percent of graduating students remaining in the region
3. History of university in the region: for those institutions established after 1975, we used all available years of operations of university or college. For those established before 1975, we used a 30-year time frame to estimate the number of alumni
4. Alumni by occupational categories are tabulated from the university-supplied data about distribution of graduates by occupation. A caveat is that this is a very general assumption that may not reflect actual occupational make-up of graduates of these universities and colleges 30 years ago and
5. BERC did not make any assumption regarding current employment status of alumni.

An estimated 234,322 alumni of Middle Tennessee higher education institutions live and work in the region. They primarily work in the areas of education, training, and library occupations; healthcare occupations; and business and financial occupations. Occupations where annual supply of graduates closely meets demand is in the areas of community and social services where 85 percent of the demand is met along with legal occupations where 79 percent of demand is met. A large divide in supply and demand is present in occupations such as buildings and grounds maintenance where less than 1 percent of demand is met by supply of graduates. In a few rare cases, the supply of graduates exceeds the demand for them. The occupations in architecture and engineering are a prime example where a 223 percent surplus exists.

Demand for Workforce and Educational Characteristics of Occupations

What is the demand for a skilled labor force in Middle Tennessee? How well do higher education institutions meet the demand for a skilled workforce? To calculate annual demand for a skilled workforce, we utilized workforce projections from the TDLWD and educational attainment by occupation from the Bureau of Labor Statistics. According to TDLWD data, the region is expected to add nearly 193,000 new jobs between 2004 and 2014. This corresponds to more than 18 percent growth in the next ten years.

These previous calculations only include job growth due to new additions. Taking into consideration job growth due to net replacement, average annual job growth is estimated to be about 37,000 new positions in Tennessee. According to BERC calculations from the BLS and TDLWD, over 12,000 of those jobs require at least a college degree; nearly 11,000 more jobs require some college and/or an Associate's degree. We must also emphasize the fact that these job growth projections and estimates do not take into account job turnovers or job changes. Although turnover rate is quite low in certain occupations, it may be well over 50 percent in certain age groups and occupations such as nursing. In addition to job turnover, this estimate does not reflect local conditions regarding aging workforce.

Taking into account average number of graduates staying in the region, the previous estimates make it clear that the 20 higher education institutions are far from meeting the demand for skilled workforce in the region. A substantial number of in-migration or other postsecondary training institutions fill the skilled workforce supply and demand gap in Middle Tennessee.

In order to understand workforce demand, it is useful to examine several perspectives. The detailed information about the certain occupations may be very useful for workforce professionals. Based on estimates from several sources, we first examine the fastest-growing occupational areas and average annual openings by level of education as ranked by numbers of jobs.

According to BERC estimates from the BLS and TDLWD, customer service, nursing, and retail occupations show the fastest growth in terms of number of jobs with each area generating more than one thousand new jobs annually in the projected decade (2004–2014). When looking at growth by percent, network systems and data communications analysts are projected to enjoy a 77 percent increase, while paralegals and legal assistants and computer software engineers are each projected to experience 53 percent growth.

What kind of education will be required of these growing occupations? Now we look at the number of jobs that may be filled by different educational attainment levels. Nearly one-third of jobs in the fastest-growing Middle Tennessee occupations require some college education, 27 percent college and higher, and the remaining high school or less than high school.

Since our primary concern in this study is to highlight the role universities and colleges play in the skilled workforce supply and demand in Middle Tennessee, we process the occupational projections data by occupations that require primarily college or above educational attainment. Many of the high growth areas, like nursing, computer software engineering, and customer service are high on the list of occupational areas that require college level education.

The occupations that primarily require at least a college education represent nearly 28 percent of total projected employment growth in Middle Tennessee adding more than 10,000 jobs annually. For instance, the nursing field is projected to generate 1,281 new jobs. Of those, only 22 will be for employees with high school or less than high school education, and the majority, 745, will require college-level education or higher. Likewise, of the 244 projected new jobs in the area of secondary education, nearly all of them, 232, will require a college level education or higher. Clearly, the occupational areas that are experiencing job growth demand greater educational attainment.

Overall, BERC estimates indicate that of more than 10,000 new job openings in these occupations, more than 73 percent require an education beyond high school, while 54 percent require at least a college degree. Only 27 percent of these jobs may be filled by individuals with a high school or less than high school education level.

Finally, we examine the occupations that are expected to experience a decline in job growth during the same decade (2004–2014). Bearing out the trend demonstrated in the earlier findings, the following estimates shows that occupations experiencing decline tend to be those that require less education.

Because of the increases in technology, many of the occupations seeing decreases in employment are those becoming obsolete. Computer operators lost 610 employees; this is more than any other occupation in the Middle Tennessee region. Mail clerks and mail machine operators except postal lost the largest percent of employment, 37 percent. It is not surprising the majority of jobs lost required high school or less than high school educational requirements.

To conclude, overall, findings indicate that demand for a college educated workforce is growing in the occupational areas that are experiencing growth, while demand for workers with a high school education or less is actually declining. In terms of meeting the demands for a skilled labor force, 20 higher education institutions are unable to meet the demand. Increasing in-migration and/or immigration of people into Middle Tennessee in recent years is partially helping to fill the gap. In addition, a variety of for-profit postsecondary training institutions is also helping meet the demand for a skilled workforce.

BUSINESS COMMUNITY—HIGHER EDUCATION INSTITUTIONS IN MIDDLE TENNESSEE

Overview

What role do higher education institutions play in the business community? This chapter presents findings from the business-interaction survey about the strategic relationships between universities and colleges and communities in Middle Tennessee. As we critically highlighted in the previous chapters, the strategic interactions among the higher education institutions and business communities constitute an essential building block of the knowledge economy. This importance comes from not only the fact that higher education institutions play a key role in supplying a skilled labor force but also their influences on broader socioeconomic dynamics, which makeup the quality of life and economic prosperity in a region.

Many studies explore the role higher education institutions play in their communities. The studies that deal with the so-called "forward linkages" focus on the effects institutes of higher education have on the business community. For example, they generate new ideas and inventions, advise and help businesses, commercialize new research findings and patents, supply a skilled labor force, and provide input to business and community leaders. Furthermore, higher education institutes cultivate tolerance and civic culture by attracting diverse groups of individuals to the region from across the world and providing an environment in which culturally diverse populations interact. They promote athletic and cultural events and improve the quality of life in the region through a multitude of venues.

Higher education institutions attract new businesses and help retain existing ones as much as they promote local business activities through many channels. Many studies cite the presence of higher education, quality of life, and the availability of a skilled labor force as three critical factors in business relocation decisions. These three factors are strongly linked to each other, but the presence of higher education institutions is foundational because it generates and perpetuates the other two factors.

In the sections that follow, we briefly review methodological issues. Next, we provide some general information about the role of universities in economic, social, and cultural areas. We finally analyze the survey results to highlight the strategic interactions among higher education institutions and communities in Middle Tennessee. A conclusion and discussion of findings will follow.

Methodology

In an attempt to address broader higher education–business interaction, BERC initiated a supplemental business-interaction survey in Middle Tennessee. The survey was distributed to 20 higher education institutions, of which 15 responded. Thirteen of these responded in some way to a supplemental business-interaction survey. Although documenting interaction between higher education and the business community is critically important for understanding the role these institutions play in the region, a lack of complete data is a limiting factor in this study.

The BERC survey asked the following major questions to higher education institutions:

1. *In what areas does your institution make the greatest contribution to economic development in Middle Tennessee?*
2. *Does your institution work closely with particular businesses? What are the reasons for your institution's involvement in those businesses?*
3. *What is the level of incentives for your staff to engage with local businesses?*
4. *How many teaching and research-related contracts were signed with businesses in the last fiscal year in Middle Tennessee?*
5. *Does your institution provide analysis, measurement, and testing services for businesses?*
6. *Does your organization have a central unit which provides business consulting?*
7. *Does your organization provide any of the following supports to spin-offs, start-ups, and/or graduate start-ups?*
8. *How responsive is your organization to skill needs and changes in labor market? Do you provide flexible businesses courses?*
9. *To what extent is your institution involved in partnerships with local and regional economic development agencies?*

We benefited from several surveys, especially British Higher Education–Business and Community Interaction survey, in designing these questions. While answering these questions provides important insights into the dynamics of the knowledge economy, the response rate to certain portions of these questions was not at the desirable level particularly because of the time frame involved in this study. As we surveyed the websites of 20 higher education institutions, we noted that many of them have programs specifically dealing with the partnership with business communities. Yet, the very same institutions were unable to respond to the similar question in the survey within the given time frame of the study. We believe that in subsequent studies the response rate will increase dramatically. What follows are the findings from the survey and BERC estimates regarding interaction between higher education institutions and the business community.

Higher Education Institutions in the Business Community

In the process of meeting their primary mission, which is to educate, Middle Tennessee's higher education institutions affect business and economic dynamics in other critical ways that improve the lives of Middle Tennessee residents. First, universities contribute a substantial amount of academic research that generates new ideas and innovations that promote business activities. In fact, universities themselves are actively involved in commercializing their innovations, investing in the community, and providing employment opportunities to many community members.

Additionally, in the process of educating the labor force, universities attract a significant number of people to the region. Many of these students are employed either by the universities or by local businesses. Each year, a substantial number of students work as interns in local businesses.

Universities can be considered export industries, as they bring a substantial amount of out-of-state money to the region. They do this through federal research grants, Pell grants and other federal scholarships for students, and out-of-state student tuition and fees. In addition, universities in Middle Tennessee often act as consultants to the business community. They promote the formation of new businesses through business incubation centers, research centers, institutes, and policy input.

Institutes of higher learning contribute to businesses and local communities via several avenues. First, they graduate an educated workforce. A total of 17,144 people obtained degrees from Middle Tennessee Higher Education Institutions in 2005. An estimated 4,607 students interned in local businesses and governments, both providing support and gaining experience that they can pass on. These institutions obtained $478 million in research funding[8] and provided 39 business incubation centers to help local businesses. Furthermore, 111 institutes and 36 research centers provided critical input to local businesses and communities.

To what extent did these higher education avenues affect the business community in 2004? The sheer size of research and inflow of substantial amount of other federal and tuition money from other regions demonstrates the extent of these institutions, contribution to the regional economy. They generated $316 million in research spending, $54 million in public service spending, $480 million in federal operating grants, $73 million in federal student grants, $274 million in student scholarships, and $463 million in investment income.

In addition to education and research avenues, institutes of higher education affect Middle Tennessee businesses and communities through campus

Table 4.4 University–Business Community Interactions: Some Indicators of Middle Tennessee Higher Education Institutions (2004)

Selected Sources of Revenues and Expenditures	Amount (Million $)	Percent in Total Expenditures
Research Spending	$315.859	10.75%
Public Service Spending	$54.118	1.84%
Federal Operating Grants	$480.074	16.34%
Federal Student Grants (including Pell)	$73.196	n/a
Total Student Scholarships	$273.614	n/a
Investment Income	$463.056	15.76%

Source: Table created by author

events. In 2005, for example, Middle Tennessee higher education institutes hosted an estimated 796 athletic events, 870 cultural events, 437 business events and 479 conferences. These campus activities along with numerous youth camps attracted at least 553,926 net new visitor days to area campuses.

Furthermore, the community benefits from more than seven million books in area libraries and nearly $134 million in estimated charitable contributions from higher education institutions and their employees. In addition to the traditional education they provide, these schools offer more than 50 online degree programs across the region serving 5,454 people, many of whom are professionals improving their skills while continuing to work. Nearly 292 people graduated from these programs in 2005.

Survey Findings

Institutional Contribution to Economic Development

The BERC survey results provide insight to how universities perceive their contributions and interactions with local businesses. First, the strongest contribution to the business community is cited in the areas of access to education, graduate retention in the region, developing local partnerships, and meeting skill needs. The weakest areas are cited in the areas of research collaboration with industry, attracting inward investment to the region, technology transfer, strategic analysis of regional economy, and spin-off activity. While the higher education community demonstrates greater desire to provide leadership for local economic development initiatives, the current level of strategic interaction in the areas of research collaboration and technology transfer seems to require additional efforts on the part of higher education communities. Just 13 out of 20 surveyed education institutions responded. Therefore, results should be interpreted accordingly.

Table 4.5   In What Areas Does Your Institution Make the Greatest Contribution to Economic Development ($N = 13$)

Area of Strength		County (%)	Middle Tennessee (%)
Strong	Access to education	100.00	53.85
Strong	Graduate retention in local region	61.54	53.85
Strong	Developing local partnerships	61.54	53.85
Strong	Meeting skill needs	61.54	53.85
Medium	Attracting nonlocal students to the region	38.46	38.46
Medium	Supporting small- and medium-sized enterprises	38.46	30.77
Medium	Support for community development	46.15	30.77
Medium	Management development	38.46	23.08
Weak	Research collaboration with industry	23.08	15.38
Weak	Attracting inward investment to region	23.08	7.69
Weak	Technology transfer	23.08	23.08
Weak	Strategic analysis of regional economy	15.38	7.69
Weak	Spin-off activity	7.69	7.69

Source: Table created by author

Close Business Interactions

As we will reveal, a considerable number of respondents work closely with businesses in health care and social assistance, finance and real estate, not-for-profit organizations, and arts, entertainment and recreation. In the manufacturing sector, businesses in machinery and computer/electronic products subsectors work closely with several higher education institutions. A moderate level of interaction takes place with businesses in accommodation and food services and government and related enterprises.

When asked why higher education institutions interacted with business sectors cited in the preceding section, 69 percent of respondents indicated the demands from businesses as a reason, 46 percent claimed expertise in the area, 39 percent cited specialization in given business areas, 31 percent indicated that they follow regional and national demands, and 15 percent cited the lack of other institutions addressing the needs in the given sector.

Research- and Testing-Related Contracts

Research- and teaching-related contracts are another avenue for interaction between institutes of higher learning and businesses. Middle Tennessee higher education institutions signed 403 contracts with businesses worth more than $25 million and involving 3,102 students and 167 businesses.

Conclusion and Discussions

While 20 higher education institutions in Middle Tennessee are involved in academic, socioeconomic, and cultural aspects of life in the region as demonstrated by the survey data, the response rate for the areas that deal with community leaderships and strategic interaction was not at the desirable level. Although the results do not represent all 20 universities, we nevertheless briefly provide information about the responses of those institutions regarding strategic community interactions.

Incentive for Faculty and Staff to Engage with Local Businesses

One area that may be promoted by higher education institutions is to provide incentives for faculty and staff to engage with local communities. According to survey results, out of seven respondents, only two institutions indicated the presence of strong incentive systems for faculty and staff engagement in the business communities.

Providing Analysis, Measurement and Testing Services, and the Presence of a Central Unit for Business Consulting

As indicated by the survey results, these two important areas are also underrepresented within the higher education communities. Out of nine respondents, only three higher education institutions provided analysis, measurement, and testing services involving 62 businesses. Furthermore, 11 higher education institutions responded to the question regarding central business for business consulting. Two of the respondents indicated that they have a central business consulting unit, which helped 72 businesses in 2005.

Business Support Services

Likewise, few institutions reported offering business support services in the form of on- and off-campus business incubators, entrepreneurship training, or business advice. Of the higher education institutions responding to this question, three provided business support in the form of one on-campus incubator, one off-campus incubator, two entrepreneurship training, and two business advice.

Responsiveness to Skill Needs

In terms of responsiveness to skill needs and changes in the labor market, a few institutions conduct rigorous analysis while some institutions only collect data without a systematic effort to realign programs. Some institutions do not monitor skill changes at all. Seven higher education institutions responded to this question. Of the seven institutions, two do not have a skill monitoring system, four collect data about skill changes but do not show systemic efforts to realign the programs, and one has sophisticated monitoring system and responds to changes in labor market demands.

Flexible Learning Environment for Businesses

In terms of providing a learning environment for businesses and professionals, a few institutions offer distance-learning for businesses and continuing work-based learning. Continuing work-based learning involved 979 individuals and generated $1.8 million. In addition, nearly half of responding institutions offer short courses for businesses either on or off campus. These courses benefited 435 individuals. Of course, we must again reiterate the fact that less than 10 higher education institutions responded to this question. Out of seven respondents, two provide distance-learning for businesses, but five indicated they do not have such a program. One higher education institution indicated the presence of continuous work-based learning system involving 979 individuals and $1.8 million in revenue. Finally, five of the nine responding higher education institutions offer on- or off-campus short business courses.

Partnership with Economic Development Agencies

Finally, BERC asked universities about the extent of their partnerships with local and regional development agencies. Five of seven responding institutions indicated that they are somewhat involved in development efforts at the senior management level. Two institutions indicated that they are very active in local and regional development efforts.

As the survey results indicate, the higher education institutions involve in regional efforts at varying capacity. Their full involvements in the areas that the BERC survey covers would create potentially powerful positive impact throughout the region. We must acknowledge in this chapter that the BERC survey has limitations in capturing the full-extent of the 20 universities involved in community affairs due to low response rate. In the future, a systematic monitoring of the business–higher education interaction may provide significant policy insights for universities, businesses, and local and state government agencies alike.

HIGHER EDUCATION INSTITUTIONS IN MIDDLE TENNESSEE FROM A COMPARATIVE PERSPECTIVE

Overview

Where does Middle Tennessee stand in relation to peer regions in the area of higher education? This chapter will address this question by analyzing higher education indicators in peer regions. Indicators of higher education provide critical insight into a region's competitive advantages. These advantages include the region's access to higher education, science and innovation, cultural diversity, and export of educational services, among others.

The broad categories of indicators we will examine include educational attainment, regional characteristics, higher education institutions, cultural diversity, research and development, science and engineering, faculty and staff, fiscal indicators, and other competitive indicators. In the sections that follow, we first briefly discuss methodological issues when analyzing diverse regions from a comparative perspective. Second, we provide a snapshot of the Middle Tennessee region in terms of educational attainment. Third, we provide a comprehensive set of indicators for the selected peer regions. Finally, we conclude with the composite rankings of regions according to these indicators.

Methodology

An analysis of regions from a comparative perspective in the area of higher education requires processing an extensive number of indicators involving a large number of universities and colleges. In constructing higher education indicators in this study, we were guided by three important principles: *consistency*, *relevancy*, and *comparability*. In addition, the *availability of data* and *time frame for the study* were two important limiting factors. We were nevertheless able to extract nearly 100 indicators that were further processed for category and composite rankings.

For *consistency*, the BERC utilized data from publicly available sources to construct indicators of higher education for peer regions. Primary data come from IPEDS. In addition to IPEDS, we also consulted the National Science Foundation, Census Bureau, and Bureau of Economic Analysis. For certain specific indicators, we utilized data from Department of Education websites for each peer region.

For *relevancy*, in identifying the indicators, the BERC took into account the broader functions of higher education institutions in a community. Therefore, we included a few environmental indicators in which higher education institutions and their communities interact. All other indicators are closely related to the broader mission of higher education institutions in a knowledge economy. Of course, the *availability* of data was critically important in the selection process.

For *comparability*, BERC used the predefined peer regions used by the Nashville Area Chamber of Commerce in its marketing efforts: Atlanta, GA; Denver, CO; Dallas, TX; Columbus, OH; Charlotte, NC; Indianapolis, IN; Raleigh, NC; Jacksonville, FL; Kansas City, MO; Louisville, KY; Richmond,

VA; and Birmingham, AL. These 12 MSAs along with Middle Tennessee region, which includes 41 counties, are used for comparison.

On many occasions, these MSAs are often used to compare performance of the Nashville MSA in certain economic areas. However, because of the focus of this study, which includes 20 higher education institutions scattered across Middle Tennessee, BERC defined the study region as Middle Tennessee instead of the Nashville MSA. Regarding the use of population or student-weighted indicators, the inclusion of the Middle Tennessee region should not cause any problems. However, this definition may pose a methodological issue in terms of comparing Middle Tennessee with the Raleigh-Cary MSA, as the research triangle region is split into two MSAs: Raleigh-Cary and Durham-Chapel Hill. In interpreting the results in this study, the reader should be aware of this boundary issue. The BERC did not attempt to redefine the regions primarily because of the time constraint for the project.

This study introduces a set of indicators in each section. For each subsection, we create several summary indicators, which are then standardized. Each region is ranked based on its relative score for a given indicator.

A Profile of Middle Tennessee

Skill Composition

In terms of educational attainment, Middle Tennessee lags behind national averages substantially. As regional economies experience structural changes in the manufacturing sector, there is a pressing need for people with higher education, defined as education beyond high school, in order to produce a competitive labor force. Middle Tennessee has a substantial surplus of low skilled workers compared to the rest of the nation while there is a major deficit of highly skilled workers.

While Middle Tennessee's skill composition is slightly higher than the state as a whole, it is still much lower than the national average. It is also significant to note that while urban counties are positioned relatively well in overall skill composition, rural counties face significant challenges in meeting the market's demand for a skilled workforce.

Science and Innovation

Science and innovation are the lifeblood of a competitive regional economy. However, this lifeblood depends on the educational attainment of a region's labor force. Using 1999 patent data, Middle Tennessee counties are analyzed in terms of patents per capita.

All of Middle Tennessee is below the national average for patents, and most of the 41 counties we examine here fall below the Tennessee average both for educational attainment and patents. The only county within the study region that exceeds the Tennessee average for patents and above average percentage of bachelor or higher degree holders is Williamson county, however, even in this case, the U.S. average is not met.

Indicators of Higher Education

In the following section, we examine 13 different indicators of higher education in 13 different peer regions, including Middle Tennessee.

Regional Characteristics

Selected characteristics of peer regions BERC used include population, income, labor force, and unemployment rate. In terms of population, the Middle Tennessee region was the fourth largest compared to its peers; however, it showed the largest increase in growth since 2000 rising nearly 14 percent. Income per capita and labor force performed poorly compared to peer regions being the bottom three in both categories. Middle Tennessee reported a slightly above-average unemployment rate.

Educational Attainment

Compared to its peers, Middle Tennessee has very low educational attainment. It has the highest percent of population with less than a high school education (28 percent) and the lowest number of college graduates holding bachelor's degrees or higher (21 percent). Looking at the Nashville MSA by itself, the city has rates of educational attainment comparable to half of the peer regions, but its overall ranking is still lower than the peer average. In terms of bachelors and above educational attainment, Raleigh (39 percent), Denver (36 percent), and Atlanta (32 percent) have the highest percentage of the population over 25 with a bachelor's degree and above.

Exporting Educational Services

In examining the net student inflow to the region's higher education institutions, we followed several steps utilizing data from a variety of sources. First, we obtained high school graduation data for each peer region by aggregating graduation data for each school jurisdiction. Then, we estimated potentially "college-bound" students utilizing educational attainment data for each region. Finally, we used IPEDS data to estimate net student inflow from other regions to each of the peer MSAs. According to BERC calculations, more than 9,500 students from other regions go to college in Middle Tennessee, making it the fourth largest exporter of educational services outside the region after Atlanta, Dallas, and Denver.

Higher Education Institutions

BERC identified 206 nonprofit (public and private) higher education institutions in these 13 regions. Given the presence of these institutions, what options do the residents of the regions have for pursuing the education programs they desire? In order to address this question, BERC calculated a summary "educational opportunity diversity" score for each region, taking into account Carnegie classifications and the highest degree offered by each institution.[9] To eliminate any bias, the summary diversity score includes the number of both institutions and students enrolled in each program area. The regions with higher diversity scores present more opportunities to their residents in terms of academic programs. Using this score, we find that Middle Tennessee and Atlanta provide more diverse educational opportunities in terms of program areas than any other peer regions.

Cultural Diversity

Another important indicator of higher education is cultural diversity. Middle Tennessee's institutions are relatively less culturally diverse than those in peer regions with the exception of Indianapolis and Columbus. One particular component of the cultural diversity score is nonresident alien enrollment. In Tennessee, nonresident alien enrollment is lower than nine of 12 peer regions. Dallas and Atlanta institutes of higher learning have the highest diversity scores.

Research and Development

The amount of research and development that universities contribute is another important indicator of the quality of higher education in a region. Middle Tennessee experienced significant growth between 2000 and 2004 in university-based research and development expenditures, but the region is still far behind Raleigh, Columbus, Birmingham, Atlanta, and Indianapolis in terms of per capita research and development spending. BERC utilized data from the National Science Foundation to calculate university-based research and development spending.

In addition to measuring the amount of money universities are spending on research and development, it is also important to look at the funding sources. A very diverse funding base indicates that a region's institutions are benefiting from a variety of sources, an indicator of success. A low diversity score indicates the region's reliance on a few sources for funding, mainly the federal government. Middle Tennessee's higher education institutions rely heavily on federal funding for research and development.

Compared to peer regions, Middle Tennessee ranks 11th out of 13 in terms of diversity of funding sources. Regions with the highest funding diversity are Raleigh, Louisville, and Columbus. Therefore, while Middle Tennessee's universities are experiencing much growth in the area of funding and research, they are not yet garnering as large a variety of funding sources as their peer regions.

Science and Engineering Graduate Students

How well is Middle Tennessee performing relative to peer regions in terms of science and engineering graduate students? This indicator is often utilized to measure a region's innovative capacity. It is, therefore, critically important to have a large number of per capita science and engineering graduate students. Unfortunately, Middle Tennessee was substantially behind other peer regions in terms of science and engineering students per capita in 2003.

In fact, only three regions—Kansas City, Charlotte, and Jacksonville—had fewer science and engineering graduate students than Middle Tennessee. Despite this low graduate number, Middle Tennessee showed an above-average increase rising more than percent from 2000.

Estimated Patents

Related to the science and engineering students as well as the presence of higher education institutions in a region is the number of patents filed. All 13 peer regions experienced a decrease in per capita patents filed between 2000 and 2005. Middle Tennessee ranks nearly in the middle of peer regions in terms of patents per capita in 2005. Indictors are estimated from statewide patent data. A region's share of patents in a state is estimated by multiplying the total patents by the ratio of the given region's college students to total college students.

Enrollment

In comparing enrollment numbers between Middle Tennessee's universities and those in peer regions, interesting trends emerge. In terms of enrollment per capita, Middle Tennessee falls in the upper half of peer region rankings. Raleigh, Richmond, Columbus, Denver, and Kansas City have higher per capita enrollment than Middle Tennessee. However, Middle Tennessee has the highest percentage of full-time students enrolled (72 percent). In addition, when we examine retention rates, Middle Tennessee universities' retention of both full-time and part-time students is higher than three-fourths of its peer region institutions.

Cost of Education

The cost of higher education is an important consideration in comparing Middle Tennessee to peer regions. First, when we look at living expenses, it is clear that Middle Tennessee institutions are relatively better suited to provide on-campus living opportunities, and the average room charge is relatively lower than those in peer regions. In terms of cost of living for out-of-state students, Middle Tennessee's universities fall somewhere in the middle of peer rankings. In this study, we only used average cost of living for out-of-state students.

How do students finance their education? In Middle Tennessee, more than 11 percent of students receive one or a combination of the following: federal grant aid, state and local grant aid, and institutional grant aid. Furthermore, nearly 7 percent of students receive loan aid, a rate higher than in most peer regions. Only Raleigh and Richmond have higher percentage of students receiving loan aid than Middle Tennessee. Unlike the case with grants, students or their parents repay loans after graduation.

When we look at the diversity of funding opportunities for students to pay for their education, we find that while Middle Tennessee higher education institutions rank second in terms of total grants per enrollee after Columbus, its diversity score ranks 12th out of 13 peer regions. This low diversity score indicates heavy reliance on a few sources, especially unfunded institutional sources. Funding source diversity scores are higher in Raleigh, Richmond, Jacksonville, and Birmingham indicating that higher education institutions in these MSAs have more balanced sources of funding for students.

Employment

A comparison of 13 regions in terms of higher education employment and functional distribution of employment follows. The average salary for higher education employees in Middle Tennessee is $51,245, very close to the average salary range for the 13 peer regions examined. The average salary presented here does not reflect cost-of-living adjustments. However, examining employment by function reveals significant differences. Only a small percentage of those Middle Tennessee employees, 22 percent, are involved primarily in instruction. Ten of the 13 peer regions rank higher than Middle Tennessee in terms of their percentages of primarily instruction-related employment. Middle Tennessee ranked third in terms of primarily research-related employment. A positive aspect of Middle Tennessee higher education employees is that many wear several hats simultaneously (as researchers, public service providers, and teachers). Considering the fundamentals of a knowledge economy, engagement of faculty and staff at different levels of community involvement is beneficial to local communities.

The weighted higher education employment data from a comparative perspective will be examined in this section. We used total number of enrollment and population as weights for employment. According to BERC and IPEDS, Middle Tennessee has the highest rate of employment per 10,000 enrollment: 2,622 faculty and staff per 10,000 students. Likewise, it has the second highest rate of employment per 10,000 people after Columbus. In Middle Tennessee, for every 10,000 people, there are 138 higher education staff and faculty members.

Sources of Revenue

In this section, we look at the sources of revenues of higher education institutions from three different perspectives: tuition and federal, state and local, and other significant sources such as investment income and gifts. Universities' revenue sources constitute another important indicator of higher education's role in a region. In fact, tuition and federal revenue sources may be considered net inflow to the region making universities an important export industry.

When examining tuition and federal sources of revenue, Middle Tennessee is either in the middle or at the lower end of the peer rankings in terms of percent share. Tuition as a source of higher education revenues accounts for 15 percent of revenue, ranking Middle Tennessee 11th out of 13 peer regions. Federal sources account for 14 percent of its revenue, ranking it fifth. However, Middle Tennessee is at the higher end of rankings in terms of per capita tuition: its tuition per enrollee is $5,294, second only to Columbus, and its federal funding per enrollee is $4,897, ranking third on the list.

Jacksonville, Denver, and Charlotte derive one-fourth of their total revenues from tuition. In terms of federal sources, Denver, Birmingham and Richmond top the list, as they have the highest percent of revenues derived from federal sources. In terms of per capita federal revenue, Birmingham receives $8,449 per enrollee, ranking first among 13 regions. Atlanta ranks second with $4,975 per enrollee.

State and local sources also provide revenue to higher education. However, both as a percentage of revenue and on a per enrollee basis, state sources do not provide a significant portion of revenue to Middle Tennessee higher education institutions. Similarly, local sources are a negligible source of income for Middle Tennessee as compared to peer region universities, contributing just $79 per enrollee, less than half a percent of revenue.

When looking at sources of revenue from a local and state perspective, we see Jacksonville, Raleigh, and Louisville derive more than one-fourth of their total revenues from the state. These MSA's revenues from the state are with $3,608; $8,260; and $4,345 per enrollee, respectively. In terms of local sources, Dallas, Kansas City, and Indianapolis top the list, as they received nearly one-tenth of their revenues from local sources with $1,702; $1,245; and $1,390 per enrollee, respectively.

Other sources of revenue, such as gifts, investment income, and auxiliary operations, represent higher education institutions' efforts to generate income. Investment income may be the result of commercialization of university inventions. Middle Tennessee institutions perform relatively better than peer regions in attracting gifts and generating investment income. In fact, Middle Tennessee ranks highest in both percentage and per capita numbers when it comes to gifts, bringing in more than two thousand dollars per enrollee. Likewise, Middle Tennessee ranks first in garnering investment income per enrollee ($4,724) and second in investment income as a percentage of revenue. Middle Tennessee's auxiliary operations rank in the middle of peer regions as a source of revenue.

Expenditures

Where do universities spend their revenue? Two areas that are critically important for a region's economy are research and public service spending. Middle Tennessee higher education institutions spend a smaller share of their income on research than peer regions; only five peer regions spend less on research. In terms of public service expenditures, Middle Tennessee's relative position is also relatively weak spending only $552 per enrollee on public service. Only two peer regions spend smaller percentages of their income on public service.

Birmingham, Atlanta and Columbus top the list in terms of per capita research expenditures with $5,544; $5,192; and $3,252 per enrollee. Birmingham, Raleigh, and Louisville have the highest per capita public services expenditures with $4,264; $1,788; and $1,331 per enrollee, respectively.

When it comes to spending on student-related areas, Middle Tennessee spends more per enrollee than most of its peer regions. On instruction, Middle Tennessee universities spend $8,425 per student, more than any other peer region. On academic support, Middle Tennessee spends $1,643 per student, ranking fifth among its peer regions. On student services, Middle Tennessee spends $1,312 per student, more than any other peer region. Overall, while

Middle Tennessee higher education institutions spend a relatively smaller share of their budgets on student-related areas, they spend a much higher amount per capita.

Conclusion and Discussions

In all, BERC compared Middle Tennessee higher education institutions to 12 peer regions using eight different categories. In ranking each region, BERC took into account nearly 100 indicators falling under eight broad categories: regional characteristics, education, R&D and science and engineering, diversity of educational opportunity, cultural diversity, enrollment and cost of education, sources of school revenues, and areas of school expenditures.

Table 4.6 Snapshot of Rankings

Ranking Categories	Middle Tennessee	Highest	Lowest
Regional Characteristics	4th	Richmond	Denver
Education	13th	Denver	Middle Tennessee
R&D and Science and Engineering	9th	Columbus	Kansas City
Diversity of Educational Opportunity	1st	Middle Tennessee	Jacksonville
Cultural Diversity	12th	Dallas	Indianapolis
Enrollment and Cost of Education	10th	Raleigh	Denver
Sources of School Revenues	1st	Middle Tennessee	Jacksonville
Expenditures	6th	Birmingham	Kansas City

Source: Table created by author

Table 4.7 Composite Rankings of the Peer Regions Based on Higher Education Indicators

MSA	Average Score	Rankings
Atlanta	0.65	1
Birmingham	0.48	8
Charlotte	0.41	11
Columbus	0.57	3
Dallas	0.54	4
Denver	0.52	5
Indianapolis	0.42	10
Jacksonville	0.39	13
Kansas City	0.44	9
Louisville	0.40	12
Middle Tennessee	0.50	7
Raleigh	0.60	2
Richmond	0.50	6

Source: Table created by author

As we highlighted each of eight broader categories and selected indicators in the previous sections, within a given category, several indicators may be moving in opposite directions. By estimating category rankings and scores, we provide a general perspective on how a region is performing compared to its peers in that given broader area such as diversity of educational opportunity. In terms of component rankings, Middle Tennessee ranks high in the areas of diversity of educational programs and diversity of revenue sources. However, the region ranks 12 out of 13 in the area of cultural diversity and at the very bottom in terms of educational attainment.

Below is a snapshot of findings from the previous section comparing Middle Tennessee's rankings with the highest (best performing) and the lowest (worst performing) regions for each of eight (8) broader categories. According to findings, the following regions appeared at least once in the highest-performing column across all categories: Middle Tennessee, Richmond, Denver, Columbus, Raleigh, Dallas, and Birmingham. The following regions were most frequently the lowest-performing MSAs: Middle Tennessee, Denver, Kansas City, Jacksonville, and Indianapolis.

Composite Rankings

Taking into account all higher education indicators, BERC's composite rankings of peer regions are as follows: Atlanta ranks first, Raleigh second, and Columbus third. Middle Tennessee ranks seventh, about average among its peers. Worst performing MSAs include: Jacksonville (last), Louisville (12th place), and Charlotte (11th place).

NOTES

1. The Presidents' Summit refers to the regular gathering of 20 university presidents in Middle Tennessee.

2. For a broader discussion of their leadership roles, see Saxenian (1996) and Perry and Wiewel (2005).

3. For a comprehensive review of some major studies about this issue, see OECD (1999).

4. For a detailed analysis of university and community interaction in Silicon Valley and Route 128, see Saxenian (1996).

5. Summarized from Murat Arik and Christian Nsiah (2004), Measuring the Economic Impact of Middle Tennessee State University, Business and Economic Research Center, Jennings A. Jones College of Business, Middle Tennessee State University (www.mtsu.edu/~berc/studies.html).

6. Visitor expenditure data for non-university-related events in Tennessee are utilized in this study. A modified version of the BERC survey of Bonnaroo Music Festival attendees is used for this purpose.

7. "Much faster growing" occupations are defined as those occupations that are expected to grow more than 27 percent between 2004 and 2014. For more information, see *Occupational Outlook Quarterly*, Spring 2006, www.bls.gov.

8. Research funding figures are from different sources and for different years.

9. We used the following standard formula to calculate "educational opportunity diversity index": $DiversityIndex = 1 - \sum p_i^2$, where ($pi$) represents the fraction of each program area in total in terms of number of institutions or total enrollment. This index is also called the Rae Index.

Chapter 5

The Nonprofit Sector in the Nashville MSA

INTRODUCTION

The nonprofit sector is an important part of both the local and national economy because it includes not only spending and associated employment, but also volunteering and civic participation in community affairs. Although its size and scope is considerable, no systematic attempt has previously been made to study this sector in the Nashville MSA. The BERC, Middle Tennessee State University, under the sponsorship of the Center for Nonprofit Management (CNM), has produced this assessment of the nonprofit sector's contribution to the local economy.

The purpose of this study is to find answers to the following questions:

1. What is the scope and size of the Nashville MSA's nonprofit sector?
2. How has the Nashville MSA's nonprofit sector evolved over the years?
3. How has the Nashville MSA's nonprofit sector managed the economic downturn?
4. How does the Nashville MSA's nonprofit sector compare with that of peer MSAs?

To answer these questions, BERC designed and administered a nonprofit survey in addition to obtaining nonprofit data from various sources. Study findings demonstrate the presence of a vibrant nonprofit sector in the Nashville MSA bringing in a significant amount of money from sources outside the Nashville MSA.

The rest of this report will proceed as follows. The second chapter deals with the review of selected literature and methodological issues. The third chapter presents a summary of the characteristics of the Nashville MSA's nonprofit sector. The fourth chapter provides a comprehensive assessment of its economic contributions. The fifth and sixth chapters compare the Nashville MSA's nonprofit sector with that of peer MSAs as well as the effect of the 2008 recession on nonprofit management.

LITERATURE REVIEW AND METHODOLOGY

How did BERC analyze the nonprofit sector's contribution to the local economy? In this section, we briefly address this question by reviewing literature, identifying data sources, and constructing the conceptual framework for data analysis.

Literature Review

Literature on the nonprofit sector deals with a wide range of topics including the economics of giving, dynamics of volunteering, management issues, civic participation, and economic impact assessments. Given the scope of this study and the research questions posed earlier, we primarily reviewed literature on the economic contributions of the nonprofit sector to the state and local economies. The selected literature reviewed for this study helped us develop consistent methodology for analyzing the nonprofit sector in the Nashville MSA. BERC consulted a mix of MSA/region-level and state-level studies. In almost all of these studies, the number of nonprofit organizations and revenues had increased. Data sources, methodology, composition, and sector size were also important factors in deciding to use these resources for developing the conceptual framework and methodology for this study.

Geography and Scope of the Nonprofit Sector

The geographical scope of this study is confined to the Nashville MSA, which includes 13 counties in Middle Tennessee: Cheatham, Dickson, Hickman, Davidson, Macon, Cannon, Sumner, Smith, Robertson, Rutherford, Trousdale, Williamson, and Wilson counties. A clearly defined study area allows us to identify out-of-area monetary flows. If the source of a nonprofit's revenue is from outside a clearly defined area, we then argue that the monetary activity is a net addition to the area's economy. This treatment is an important component of the economic impact estimates in the following sections.

Does this study include all nonprofit organizations?

Consistent with the literature, this study deals with a selected number of nonprofit organizations. BERC initially used the IRS classification of tax-exempt institutions. BERC collected information for institutions classified under the following subgroups: Public Charities (501(c)(3)), Civic Leagues and Social Welfare Organizations (501(c)(4)), and Business Leagues (501(c)(6)). In choosing nonprofits for this survey, BERC used the nonprofits' income as a main criterion under the following guideline: if the last reported income (IRS 990 form) was less than $25,000, BERC excluded that organization. Furthermore, consistent with the literature, churches were excluded.

Economic Impact Definition and IMPLAN Software

What is the concept of economic impact, and how do we estimate it? In analyzing the nonprofit sector, BERC provides three types of assessment: (I) its economic impact (narrow category); (II) its economic contribution (broader category); and (III) its economic contribution including volunteer hours (the broadest category).

Economic Impact and Economic Contributions

Economic impact refers to economic activities that are net new additions to the local economy. Such activities include exporting of goods and services by local businesses to areas outside the Nashville MSA, out-of-area visitor spending, and recapturing of economic activities sent outside the Nashville MSA due to lack of local business services. In the case of the nonprofit industry, we measure the direct economic impact by identifying the amount of monetary flow to the study region from outside the Nashville MSA: the net contributions to local economic activities. Without these nonprofit organizations, the local economy would have been smaller in proportion to the net new economic activities associated with the nonprofit sector as well as their indirect and induced effects.

This study makes a distinction between economic impact and economic contributions. While the former refers to new economic activity, the latter deals with the total size of the nonprofit sector in the Nashville MSA. The concept of economic contributions then refers to total spending of the nonprofit sector in the local economy. Because it is a broader concept, any measure of economic contributions includes the economic impact measures. To measure the economic contributions, this study first calculates total expenditure of the nonprofit sector and then *counterfactually* removes the sector from the local economy to identify indirect and induced effects.

Finally, this study argues that the economic activities associated with the nonprofit sector would not have been possible with only their given level of employment and nothing more. Volunteers are critically important in this sector. In a third category, this study quantifies total wages associated with volunteer labor and adds the total direct wages to the economic-contribution estimates.

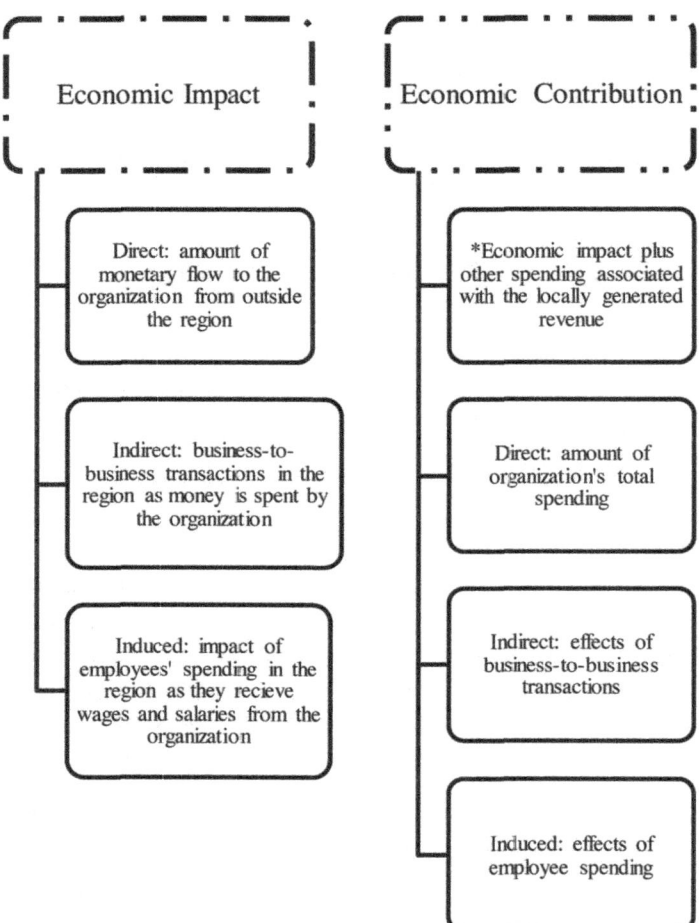

Figure 5.1 Determining Economic Impact and Economic Contribution. *Source*: Figure created by author

IMPLAN Model

To estimate *indirect* and *induced* effects of economic activities, BERC uses the model developed for the Nashville MSA. IMPLAN is a nationally recognized, commonly used input-output model to measure the economic and fiscal effects of economic development projects.

What is this Study not Measuring?

It is important to note that by its very nature, this study estimates economic contributions of the nonprofit organizations' spending in the Nashville MSA. This estimate is markedly different from the economic contributions of nonprofit-related economic activities in the Nashville MSA. In the latter case, a study would also estimate any economic activity associated with a nonprofit organization. For example, while this research study focuses simply on the impact of a university's operating expenditure spending, a broader study might also include spending associated with visitors to the campus, students' spending, capital expenditures, etc. Adding all of these components could even double the total impact estimate of an organization's operating expenditure. For this reason, the results in this study are not directly comparable with studies that deal with all economic activities associated with a nonprofit organization.

Data and Data Sources

Where did the data originate? This study has used multiple sources to construct the input database. Figure 5.2 below summarizes the process followed to estimate the variables of interest.

Data Identification and Extraction Process

BERC created several databases used in this study. At the regional level, establishment, employment, revenue, and population indicators were collected to standardize the nonprofit indicators across peer MSAs. Using the National Center for Charitable Statistics (NCCS) Core Files, BERC staff identified several outlier organizations in the database and collected employment and volunteering information for those organizations using IRS 990 form files.

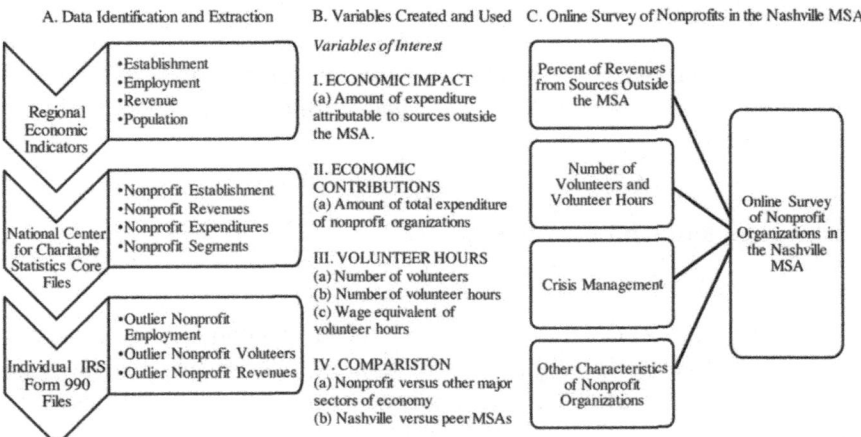

Figure 5.2 Database Identification, Survey Administration, and Indicator Creation Process. *Source*: Figure created by author

Online Survey of Nonprofits in the Nashville MSA

BERC designed and administered an online survey of nonprofit organizations in February 2013. The primary purpose was to gather several pieces of information that would supplement the data BERC obtained in the previous sections. BERC received 306 completed surveys from nonprofit organizations out of 1,086 organizations surveyed for a survey response rate of 28.18 percent. The survey helped us answer three major questions:

1. What is the percent of nonprofit revenues coming from sources outside the Nashville MSA?
2. What is the extent of volunteering in the Nashville MSA?
3. How did nonprofit organizations manage the 2008 recession?

In the section that follows, we will cover these issues extensively.

Variables Created and Used in This Study

As a result of the processes in sections prior, BERC created several variables that will be used throughout this study (See Figure 5.1).

CHARACTERISTICS OF THE NONPROFIT SECTOR AND THE NASHVILLE MSA ECONOMY

Organizations in the nonprofit sector represent a diverse group of the NAICS (North American Industrial Classification System) sectors in the regional economy. They also differ in size in terms of employment, revenue, and expenditure. For example, the 15 largest organizations in the Nashville MSA's nonprofit sector account for two-thirds of its total revenue and expenditure. This section explores the dynamics of the nonprofit sector in the Nashville MSA.

Size, Scope and Change by Segment

Nonprofit Establishments

According to the NCCS Core Files, the number of nonprofit organizations whose total revenue is larger than $25,000 was 2,045 in the Nashville MSA in fiscal year 2010–2011 representing 5 percent of all businesses in the Nashville MSA. In terms of nonprofit organizations by major segment, the human services segment is by far the largest, representing 34 percent of all nonprofits. Falling behind are the public and social benefit segment along with the education segment accounting 20 percent and 18 percent of nonprofit organizations in the Nashville MSA, respectively. Compared with 2008, the number of nonprofit organizations increased by 5 percent, while the total number of businesses in the Nashville MSA decreased by 3 percent.

Changes in the number of nonprofit organizations in the Nashville MSA from 2008 to 2010 were also examined. The largest growth occurred in the *international* segment, with an increase of 39 percent to 46 in 2010. In terms of the absolute number, the segments of *human services* and *education* added 44 and 31 new organizations, respectively. Organizations classified under mutual benefit, public and societal benefit, and unknown were either stagnant or experienced decline in numbers between 2008 and 2010.

Nonprofit Revenues

What is the size of the nonprofit sector in the Nashville MSA? To estimate this figure, BERC used a consistent source, the NCCS Core Files, and an online survey. This report presents a conservative estimate of total revenue because BERC excluded (a) all organizations with less than $25,000 in annual revenue and (b) about 400 smaller organizations because the mailed surveys were returned as undeliverable.

According to BERC estimates, the size of the nonprofit sector in the Nashville MSA was $9.4 billion in 2010. The nonprofit sector experienced significant growth between 2008 and 2010, with a 10 percent increase in revenue in current dollars.

How is this Revenue Distributed across Major Nonprofit Segments?

The breakdown of nonprofit sector revenue by major segment is detailed below. The education segment accounts for nearly half (47 percent) of nonprofit revenues with $4.4 billion. The second-largest segment is health care with $3.1 billion and a 33 percent share, followed by human services with $0.94 billion and public and societal benefits with $0.62 billion.

All major nonprofit segments recorded growth in revenue between 2008 and 2010. While some segments recorded moderate growth in terms of percent change, segments such as mutual benefit, international, and those classified as unknown doubled their revenues.

Nonprofit Expenditures

What matters for this study is how much money nonprofit organizations spend in the Nashville MSA. The amount of money these organizations spend enters as a direct input into the regional IMPLAN model to measure the economic contributions of these organizations. BERC used the NCCS Core Files and online survey results to calculate the expenditure side of the equation. As stated in the methodology section, *this study does not attempt to measure capital expenditures because these expenditures may show significant annual fluctuations.*

According to BERC estimates, total expenditure of the nonprofit sector in the Nashville MSA was $8.97 billion in 2010. The nonprofit sector's expenditure showed significant growth between 2008 and 2010 with an 11 percent increase in expenditures in current dollars.

How is this Expenditure Distributed across Major Nonprofit Segments?

A summarized breakdown of nonprofit sector expenditure by major segment follows. The education segment of the nonprofit sector, with $4.3 billion, accounts for nearly half (48 percent) of nonprofit expenditures. The second-largest segment is health care with $3.0 billion and a 33 percent share, followed by human services with $0.90 billion and public and societal benefits with $0.51 billion.

Unlike the case of nonprofit revenue, a few nonprofit segments recorded a decline in total expenditures between 2008 and 2010: the mutual benefit segment experienced an 8 percent decline, and the public and societal benefit segment experienced a 5 percent decline in expenditures. Total decline in these segments amounted to nearly $29 million. On the other hand, the education and health care segments recorded significant expenditure growth (in absolute size) with a combined total growth of $0.79 billion.

Nonprofit Employment

How many people are employed by this diverse group of nonprofit organizations? To answer this question, BERC directly asked nonprofit organizations for feedback through an online survey. In addition, BERC did a separate analysis of the 12 largest outlier organizations to get their employment figure separately. According to BERC estimates, nonprofit organizations have 140,650 full-time and 40,489 part-time employees with a combined full-time equivalent (FTE) of 151,734 employees. Direct employment figures represent nearly 15 percent of Nashville MSA employment.

Given the strength of the health care sector in the Nashville MSA, it is not surprising that the health care segment leads all others by 68,218 employees. Education is second with 52,066 and human services a distant third with 20,502 employees. In this context, it is important to highlight the fact that unlike many peer MSAs, the education and health care segments in the Nashville MSA nonprofit sector are very much intertwined because of the presence of both Vanderbilt University and Meharry Medical College.

Nonprofit employment in the Nashville MSA is broken into 9 segments. The health care segment represents nearly 45 percent of nonprofit sector employment, followed by education (34 percent) and human services (14 percent). Overall, direct employment by the nonprofit sector is a major force in the Nashville MSA. These estimates do not include the volunteer force these organizations mobilize when there is an unmet need in society.

Nonprofit Volunteers

BERC administered an online survey to measure the level of volunteer activities in the nonprofit sector of the Nashville MSA. According to BERC estimates, a total of 429,588 people volunteered for nonprofit organizations in 2011. Since this survey was not a survey of the population about its volunteering activities, this number may involve duplicate counts of certain individuals volunteering for several organizations throughout the year.

What does this tell us about the extent of volunteering in the Nashville MSA?

Assuming this number represents unique individuals, one in every three people over 16 years of age volunteered in the nonprofit sector in the Nashville MSA in 2011. This figure is somewhat higher than U.S. figures measured through the Current Population Survey (www.bls.gov): According to the September 2012 estimates, slightly over one in every four individuals over 16 years of age had volunteered in the U.S. in 2011.

What is the significance of volunteering in the Nashville MSA? According to BERC estimates, the volunteers in the Nashville MSA recorded 15,641,448 hours of volunteering in 2011. If we use full-time (40 hours per week) employment figures, these volunteer hours translate into 8,147 full-time employment equivalency. When we use the 2011 average annual wage for a full-time nonfarm employee in the Nashville MSA, $46,150, the nonprofit volunteering's monetary value is $376 million.

When analyzing the segments most impacted by volunteers, a few stick out. The human services segment leads with 225,953 volunteers (53 percent of all volunteers), followed by public and societal benefit. The public and societal benefit segment has the largest number of volunteer hours with 5.9 million and full-time employment equivalents with 3,056. Public and societal benefit made up 38 percent of total volunteer hours and volunteer full-time equivalency.

Nonprofits as an Export Base

One of the critical research goals of this study is to identify the amount of money flowing to the Nashville MSA from outside sources. BERC used an

Table 5.1 Volunteering and the Nonprofit Sector in the Nashville MSA (2011)

Nonprofit Segment	Volunteers (People)	Volunteer Hours	Volunteer FTE Equivalency
Arts	18,401	1,212,556	632
Education	37,299	314,686	164
Environment and Animals	13,317	412,932	215
Health Care	33,759	875,907	456
Human Services	225,953	5,144,743	2,680
International	10,166	1,811,664	944
Mutual Benefit	0	0	0
Public and Societal Benefit (Other)	90,601	5,866,704	3,056
Unknown	92	2,256	1
Total	429,588	15,641,448	8,147

Source: Table created by author.

online survey to identify the percent of nonprofit revenues flowing from sources outside the Nashville MSA. From the survey results, we then estimated the total amount of nonprofit expenditure associated with outside sources. This amount is the net new addition to the study region's economy on which economic impact estimates are based.

Survey results indicate nearly 20 percent of nonprofit organizations in the Nashville MSA have received more than 50 percent of their revenues from sources outside the study region. By using mid-point values, BERC estimated that $2.7 billion in 2011 flowed into the Nashville MSA economy from outside sources because of nonprofit sector activities. In 2008, the total amount of that flow was estimated at $2.5 billion. The amount of money flowing into the Nashville MSA from other regions grew by 8 percent between 2008 and 2011.

What does this figure tell us about the nonprofit sector's role in the Nashville MSA economy? The nonprofit sector is like an export sector bringing a significant amount of money into the region by selling goods and services to individuals both inside and outside of the Nashville MSA. In 2011, an estimated 29 percent of all nonprofit revenues flowed from other regions. This figure was similar in 2008. Given the margin of error in the survey, it would be reasonable to state that one in every three dollars of nonprofit revenues comes from other regions.

How is the export base of nonprofit revenue distributed across major nonprofit segments? According to the BERC survey, the international segment of nonprofit organizations attracts the largest share, 45 percent, of its revenues from other regions, followed by the public and societal benefit (32 percent) and the health care segment (30 percent). In terms of the actual dollar amount, education at $1.27 billion, health care at $0.92 billion, and human services at $0.22 billion occupy the top three positions. Compared to 2008, all segments except health care recorded at least a double- or triple-digit growth rate in revenues coming from other regions in the most recent fiscal year. Over the years, the education segment's share in the total export base increased more than one percentage point (to 47 percent), while the health care segment lost nearly three percentage points (dropping to 35 percent).

Export-base calculations in this section will inform us in the following sections about the size of the total economic impact of the nonprofit sector in the Nashville MSA. Following a brief comparative data analysis of the Nashville MSA's nonprofit sector, the economic and fiscal impacts, as well as total contributions of nonprofits and volunteering, will be presented.

The Nonprofit Sector and the Nashville MSA Economy

In the previous section, we highlighted the fact that the nonprofit sector represents about 15 percent of total employment in the Nashville MSA. The nonprofit sector's revenue represents 7 percent of the Nashville MSA's business revenue (output) and 6 percent of total businesses.

How does it compare with the other major sectors in the Nashville MSA economy if we treat the nonprofit sector as an independent major economic sector in the Nashville MSA? In terms of employment share in the Nashville MSA economy, the sector would become number one with a little over 15 percent in front of government and non NAICs and health and social services which each make up 11 percent of the employment share.

The nonprofit sector's share is somewhat smaller in terms of business revenue being the fifth best in the region and accounting for 7 percent of the regional output. In terms of GDP, the nonprofit sector is the third highest producer accounting for 11 percent of the region's total value added.

Compared with the major sectors in the regional economy, the nonprofit sector emerges as an economic powerhouse in terms of direct employment. The next section looks at additional dynamics to explore what other jobs, revenue, income, and taxes are associated with this direct employment.

ECONOMIC ASSESSMENT OF THE NONPROFIT SECTOR

As the previous chapter clearly establishes, the nonprofit sector in the Nashville MSA is already a sizable sector. In this section, we explore the indirect and induced contribution of the nonprofit sector to the regional economy. For the analysis, we use the IMPLAN model, created for the study region with data from our online survey results and NCCS Core Files. We explore three concepts (economic impact, economic contributions, and economic contributions plus volunteering) along three major dimensions (direct, indirect, and induced effects).

Economic Impact—Export Component

What is the meaning of economic impact? Economic impact refers to an economic activity's net new contribution to the region in which the activity takes place. Some examples include a visitor from out of town spending money on a hotel/motel, a new manufacturing plant operating in the region, federal or out-of-region money flowing to an area to support a new program, or an activity that is unique to the region. Economic impact analysis is different from economic contributions or economic significance analysis, in which we often counterfactually remove an institution, program, or event from an economy without determining whether that given institution, program, or event may be considered a net new addition to the region. This section will analyze the economic impact of the nonprofit sector on the Nashville MSA economy.

How is the direct economic impact figure determined? BERC used an online nonprofit survey to capture what percent of nonprofit revenue flows from sources outside the study region. This estimate gives a conservative figure regarding resource flow to the region from outside sources. Many nonprofit organizations may provide a unique service to the study area residents. In certain medical fields, there may not be even close substitutes within the Nashville MSA. However, making an assessment of each organization's unique contribution to the region is beyond the scope of this project. Therefore as a conservative estimate, the economic impact assessment in this study focuses on the amount of funding flowing to Nashville from other regions.

In reporting economic impact and economic-contribution estimates, we follow the procedure outlined below:

1. *Business revenue (output) effect:* direct, indirect (the effect of business-to-business interactions), and induced (the effect of employee spending of wages and salaries) by nonprofit segment and major industries. These measures (indirect and induced) are also called the ripple effect. The business revenue effect represents all economic activities (i.e., trades, value added, income, taxes, proprietary income, etc.) associated with the activity. Therefore, this figure should not be aggregated with any other measures reported here.
2. *Employment effect:* direct, indirect, and induced by nonprofit segment and major industries.
3. *Labor income effect:* direct, indirect, and induced by nonprofit segment and major industries.
4. *Local and state taxes:* total taxes by nonprofit segment.

In this context, it is also important to remember the major assumptions used for this section:

1. The study region is the Nashville MSA—13 counties in Middle Tennessee.
2. Only nonprofit organizations registered under 501(c)(3), 501(c)(4), and 501(c)(6) are included. As a further step, all churches are excluded.
3. Only organizations with an annual revenue of $25,000 and above are included.
4. In the economic impact section, only the component of revenue flowing to the Nashville MSA from outside sources is included.
5. No further assumptions regarding the substitution effect, recapture rate, or any other attributes of nonprofit organizations have been made.
6. Data sources are the NCCS Core Files for screening purposes and total nonprofit revenue and the BERC online nonprofit survey for an average percent of revenue flowing from outside the Nashville MSA.
7. There may be a certain degree of discrepancy in data files in terms of number of establishments, revenue, expenditure, and employment, resulting from
   a. the use of multiple databases
   b. several levels of aggregation and
   c. change in data year and impact year (e.g., the NCCS Core Files are primarily for the year 2010–2011; we deflated these numbers to 2011 to align with survey estimates).

Economic Impact by Segment

Business Revenue

Nonprofit organizations' total economic impact in the Nashville MSA, measured as business revenue, is $6.12 billion. This represents 4 percent of the Nashville MSA's total output (business revenue) in 2011. In FY 2011, activities associated with nonprofit organizations accounted for $201 million in state and local taxes.

Which Segment's Impact is the Largest?

The education segment generated the largest economic impact among nonprofits with nearly $3 billion in 2011. The critical player in this segment is Vanderbilt University. The health care segment is next with a $2.1 billion economic impact on the Nashville MSA economy. For every direct dollar spent by nonprofit organizations, an additional $1.22 was created in the greater Nashville economy. This is primarily because much of the organizational spending in the education and health care segments is in the form of salary and wages.

Employment

What is the net employment impact of the nonprofit sector on the Nashville MSA economy? The total employment impact of the nonprofit sector on the Nashville MSA economy is 72,095 jobs. This figure accounts for 7 percent of all jobs in the Nashville MSA. For every 100 *direct* nonprofit jobs, an additional 55 jobs are created in the Nashville MSA. The largest nonprofit segment by employment impact is health care with 29,700 total jobs (direct, indirect, and induced). The education segment follows closely with 28,863, and the human services segment occupies third place with 6,852.

Although some nonprofit segments have a lesser employment impact, in some cases this may be due to two issues related to the study's methodology:

1. many small organizations in the arts and other segments may be excluded because they do not satisfy the $25,000 income minimum, and
2. many small organizations rely on volunteer labor to operate.

Wages and Salaries

How much money do people earn because of the nonprofit sector in the Nashville MSA? In FY 2011, nonprofit sector–related economic activities account for $2.7 billion in wages and salaries representing nearly 5 percent of the Nashville MSA's total wages and salaries. For every dollar of direct wages and salaries, an additional $0.91 of wages and salaries was created in the Nashville MSA. Four major segments account for this sizable impact on wages and salaries: education with $1.3 billion, health care with $0.92 billion, human services with $0.22 billion, and public and societal benefit with $0.19 billion.

Economic Impact by Major Industries

Business Revenue

The largest sectors impacted by the nonprofit sector in the Nashville MSA are other services, health and social services, finance and insurance, educational services, real estate and rental, and professional-scientific and technical services. These six sectors receive 78 percent of business revenue impacts leaving the remaining 22 percent, $1.4 billion, to be split between the remaining 14 sectors.

Employment

The results here are similar to the business revenue impact: the largest two major sectors are other services and health and social services. The educational services industry ranks third. These three sectors receive 68 percent or 49,200 of the 72,095 jobs.

To conclude, the economic impact of the Nashville MSA nonprofit sector is significant, accounting for nearly 5 percent of employment and wages and salaries and 4.4 percent of total business revenue (output). In terms of total impact, if nonprofit organizations were not operating in the region, the Nashville MSA would have lost $6.12 billion in business revenue, 72,095 jobs, and $2.7 billion in wages and salaries. In the next section, this study takes a broader perspective and analyzes total contributions of the nonprofit sector to the Nashville MSA economy.

Economic Contributions—Total Spending

This section answers the following question: What is the true size of the nonprofit sector in the Nashville MSA? To answer this question, BERC estimated total expenditure of the nonprofit sector by nonprofit segment, major industry, and IMPLAN codes. BERC then counterfactually removed the nonprofit sector from the model to estimate indirect, induced, and state and local tax impacts. We would like to caution the reader about the conceptual difference between an economic impact and an economic contribution. In the latter case, some portions of activities, goods, and services might still be provided by other agencies or individuals without much loss to the local economy if nonprofit organizations providing those goods and services ceased to exist. In reporting the contributions of the nonprofit sector to the local economy, we follow a similar format to the one outlined under the economic impact section.

Business revenue. What is the total contribution of the nonprofit sector to the Nashville MSA economy? How much money do these nonprofits spend in the local economy? How does total nonprofit revenue (direct + indirect + induced) compare with total business revenue in the Nashville MSA? Which nonprofit sector contributes the most to the local economy? How much state and local tax revenue is generated by the operations of the Nashville MSA's nonprofit sector? These are the major questions this section addresses.

Economic Contributions by Segment

Business revenue

A total of $9.3 billion (in 2011 $) in direct spending generates additional revenue of $11.3 billion in the local economy. This means that for every dollar of money spent by the nonprofit sector, an additional $1.21 is created through the ripple effect. Total contribution of the nonprofit sector to the local economy is $20.53 billion, representing 15 percent of the Nashville MSA's total business revenue. Total taxes associated with nonprofit spending are $0.68 billion in the Nashville MSA. When reviewing nonprofits' contribution to the local economy, keep in mind that Vanderbilt University with its educational and medical components, Meharry Medical College, Belmont University, and several other colleges and hospitals are included in the analysis.

Which nonprofit segments contribute most to the local economy? According to BERC estimates, education, health care, and human services segments are the top three contributors. Education accounted for nearly 49 percent, or $10 billion, of total business revenues. This is followed by health care, contributing $7 billion, and human services, contributing $2 billion.

Employment

The findings for employment contribution suggests the nonprofit sector's presence in the Nashville MSA economy is significant. The total employment contribution of the nonprofit sector to the Nashville MSA economy is 237,820 jobs. This figure represents nearly one in every four jobs in the Nashville MSA economy. Education and health care contribute around 95,000 jobs each to the local economy. According to these estimates, every 100 direct jobs associated with the nonprofit sector generates an additional 57 jobs through multipliers.

Wages and Salaries

How much money are people earning annually because of the nonprofit sector in the Nashville MSA? This amount is $8.96 billion. In fiscal year 2011, the operation of nonprofit organizations accounted for 17 percent of Nashville MSA wages and salaries. Following the pattern established in previous sections, education accounts for $4 billion, almost half, of all wages and salaries contributed by the nonprofit sector in the Nashville MSA. Additional sectors receiving significant contributions are health care ($3 billion) and human services ($0.89 billion).

For every dollar of direct wages and salaries paid by the nonprofit sector, an additional $0.90 is generated in the study area through multipliers. The largest nonprofit segments are education, health care, and human services.

Economic Contribution by Major Industry

Business Revenue

A caveat is in order regarding the comparison of business revenue contribution with the nonprofit segments: the nonprofit education segment is different from the education sector under the NAICS classification; one organization may be designated under the nonprofit education segment, but it may be operating under the *other services* sector of the NAICS industry classification. Other services, health and social services, and education are the largest industries associated with the nonprofit sector in the Nashville MSA.

Employment

Employment contributions of the nonprofit sector to the Nashville MSA economy total 237,820 jobs in FY 2011. For this segment, BERC used two data streams: data derived from the regional IMPLAN model and BERC estimates based on the nonprofit survey. Findings show health and social services, other services, and educational services receive the most jobs as a result of the nonprofit sector. These sectors receive 77,253; 54,500; and 31,194 jobs, respectively, as a result of direct, indirect, and induced contributions.

To conclude, the nonprofit sector's contribution to the Nashville MSA economy is substantial. Because the nonprofit sector is so diverse, it affects all aspects of economic activity within the study region. The next section deals with the volunteering effect on the Nashville MSA economy.

Economic Contributions plus Volunteering

When we talk about nonprofit organizations, the first thing that comes to mind is volunteering. What role does volunteering play in regional economic activity? This section presents three views in analyzing volunteers' contribution to economic activity:

1. *Volunteers as an addition to the total contributions of nonprofits to the regional economy.* In this case, we estimate the wage equivalency of volunteering activities and add the monetary value to the total contributions. Since volunteers do not get paid, they do not have indirect and induced economic impact.
2. *Volunteers as enablers.* In this view, volunteers make a tremendous contribution to the economy. A portion of the economic contribution of nonprofit organizations identified in the previous section was possible only because of the presence of a large number of volunteers. In this sense, part of the total contribution should be recalculated to show the impact of volunteering.
3. *A hybrid view that takes into account the first two arguments.* This paper uses this approach to identify the effect of volunteering in the nonprofit sector on the Nashville economy.

To recap, the estimated value of volunteering is 8,147 FTEs in the Nashville MSA. Many small organizations are simply run by volunteers. What would be the business revenue, labor income, and employment equivalency of actually employing 8,147 FTE volunteers and diverting resources of nonprofits to pay these individuals? Because of volunteer hours, nonprofit organizations were able to generate nearly $0.72 billion worth of economic activities, 8,147 jobs, and $307 million in wages and salaries. The sector of public and societal benefit and human services are the most impacted by volunteer efforts. In the literature we reviewed, numerous studies repeatedly mentioned that the survival of many organizations would not be possible without volunteers.

BERC estimated the total value of volunteering as an enabling and additive concept. According to our calculations, volunteering is a billion-dollar business in the Nashville MSA, some of which (the enabler segment) was already accounted for in the economic-contribution analysis in the previous section. The impact of volunteering on employment and labor income (enabling and additive) is 16,294 jobs and $683 million, respectively.

After advancing the value of volunteering as an additive concept and integrating it into the broader economic-contribution estimates, we see increases in the amount of economic contributions. Including volunteering results in nearly $21 billion in business revenue, 246,000 jobs, and $9.3 billion in labor income.

To summarize, volunteering is a major force in the local economy, allowing many nonprofit organizations to survive without full-time employees. Volunteers should be treated as both enablers and additive to the economic-activity base. Volunteers allow the current level of nonprofit-related economic activity to occur. Without them, there would not be enough resources to carry out an important portion of nonprofit-related economic activity. The in-kind nature of volunteering should be recognized, quantified, and included in a contribution analysis as presented in this study.

RECESSION CRISIS MANAGEMENT AND NONPROFITS IN THE NASHVILLE MSA

BERC administered an online survey in February 2013 to analyze how the 2008 recession affected nonprofit organizations. This section presents the findings from this survey.

Overall Impact of Crisis

How did the 2008 recession affect nonprofit revenue? The effect of the 2008 recession on nonprofit institutions was not uniform. Nearly half of the surveyed organizations indicated that the recession decreased their revenue. One in every three organizations maintained the same level of revenue during the recession, while 16 percent of respondents increased their revenue during this crisis period.

Regarding the demand side of the equation, nearly 56 percent of survey respondents recorded an increase in demand for their services. Only 11 percent indicated that demand for their services decreased because of the recession. It is clear that the recession created a difficult situation for many nonprofits: as the demand for their services increased, their revenue to meet those demands decreased.

How did these nonprofits manage the impact of the recession? Nearly 83 percent of respondents took some sort of action to respond to the recession. A little over 13 percent reduced services offered, 20 percent reduced employment/hours, 20 percent increased volunteer hours, and 29 percent took some other action.

Nearly one-third (29 percent) of those organizations citing an action under the "other" category mentioned efficiency, cost-cutting measures, or restructuring as a primary action. Adjusting the organization's budget and also seeking and obtaining new funds were cited as the second most important actions.

In response to the recession, has your organization attempted to use any of the following strategies? As this was a follow-up to the previous question, responses were not that surprising. Nearly one-third of the respondents took action to reduce operating costs, one-fifth implemented strategic planning and management, and 15 percent increased volunteering. Those organizations that mentioned the "other" category mirrored the responses and concerns discussed above.

What is the outlook for the next six to twelve months in terms of revenue and demand for services? Nearly three-fifths of nonprofit organizations expect their revenues to increase in that time. About 10 percent see a reduced revenue outlook. Nearly one-third of respondents expect their organizations' revenues to remain the same.

When asked the outlook for demand in the next 6 to 12 months, virtually all organizations agree that demand for services will either remain the same or increase. Nearly 71 percent expect to see an increase in demand for their services. Less than one percent expected demand to decrease.

Nonprofit organizations have felt the impact of the economic downturn starting in 2007. While the majority were affected negatively and forced to develop strategies to mediate the negative impact, a few of these organizations experienced positive growth in both demand for services and revenues.

A COMPARATIVE PERSPECTIVE ON THE NONPROFIT SECTOR IN THE NASHVILLE MSA

How does the Nashville MSA compare with peer MSAs in terms of selected nonprofit indicators? To make the comparison, BERC selected 10 peer MSAs

Table 5.2 Socioeconomic and Nonprofit Characteristics of Peer MSAs in 2010

	Population	Employment	Establishments	GDP*	Nonprofit Revenue**	Nonprofit Expenditure**
Birmingham, AL	1,129,068	642,821	25,686	$52.554	$4.577	$4.448
Charlotte, NC	1,763,969	1,063,731	44,513	$113,861	$6.776	$6.362
Columbus, OH	1,840,584	1,162,188	39,286	$91,295	$10.969	$10.241
Indianapolis, IN	1,760,826	1,090,538	42,317	$100,837	$12.603	$11.794
Jacksonville, FL	1,348,702	783,003	34,085	$59,262	$6.401	$6.034
Kansas City, MO	2,039,766	1,253,279	50,129	$106,006	$10.417	$10.252
Louisville, KY	1,285,891	744,413	29,859	$57,340	$8.056	$7.838
Nashville, TN	1,594,885	991,981	37,619	$82,369	$9.199	$8.838
Raleigh, NC	1,137,297	654,958	28,933	$56,305	$13.231	$12.383
Richmond, VA	1,260,396	758,181	31,037	$64,740	$3.750	$3.660

*In Millions of current dollars
**In Billions of current dollars
Source: Table created by author

widely used by the Nashville Area Chamber of Commerce in their publications. They include Birmingham, AL; Charlotte, NC; Columbus, OH; Indianapolis, IN; Jacksonville, FL; Kansas City, MO; Louisville, KY; Nashville, TN; Raleigh, NC; and Richmond, VA. BERC especially focused on the peers with similar population size. The selected characteristics of these peers are presented in Table 5.2.

BERC obtained nonprofit data from NCCS Core Files. Among the peer MSAs, the largest total revenue is recorded in Raleigh, followed by Indianapolis, Columbus, and Kansas City. The Nashville MSA is virtually in the middle of the group, occupying fifth place. Columbus has the largest number of nonprofit establishments, followed by Indianapolis, Raleigh, and Kansas City. Again, Nashville occupies fifth place.

In order to get a better picture of the peer MSAs, BERC used several standardized indicators and ranked each MSA by its score on each. The following indicators were used: (1) nonprofit establishments as a percent of total MSA businesses, (2) nonprofit revenue as a percent of gross regional product (GDP), (3) nonprofit revenue per capita, (4) nonprofit expenditure per capita, (5) the establishment diversity index (whether or not establishments are concentrated in a few segments of the nonprofit sector), (6) the revenue diversity index, and (7) the expenditure diversity index. To calculate the diversity index by each indicator, BERC used 10 major segments of the nonprofit sector excluding religion-related organizations (only churches).

Table 5.3 presents findings of this exercise. In terms of nonprofit establishments as a percent of total businesses, Raleigh ranks first with 9 percent, Columbus ranks second with 8 percent, and Indianapolis ranks third with 6 percent. Nashville ranks sixth with 5 percent. For nonprofit revenue as a share in GDP, Raleigh and Louisville take first and second place, while

Table 5.3 Nonprofit Indicators from a Comparative Perspective: Nashville and Its Peers

Rank of Nonprofit:	% in Total Establishments	Revenue as % in GDP	Revenue per Capita	Expenditure per Capita	Diversity Index			Average Rank
					Establishment	Revenue	Expenditure	
Raleigh, NC	1	1	1	1	1	1	1	1
Indianapolis, IN	3	3	2	2	7	6	5	2
Nashville, TN	6	5	5	5	4	3	3	3
Columbus, OH	2	4	4	4	10	4	4	4
Richmond, VA	4	10	10	10	2	2	2	5
Kansas City, MO	5	7	6	6	6	5	6	6
Louisville, KY	7	2	3	3	8	10	10	7
Birmingham, AL	8	8	8	8	5	7	7	8
Jacksonville, FL	10	6	7	7	3	9	9	9
Charlotte, NC	9	9	9	9	9	8	8	10

Source: Table created by author

Nashville ranks fifth. In other categories, Nashville's ranking does not change much, occupying the fifth spot. However, in terms of diversity, Nashville ranks third after Raleigh and Richmond. This relatively better ranking suggests that the distribution of nonprofit resources in Nashville across nonprofit segments is relatively better than most peer MSAs. Overall, Nashville ranks third among the peer MSAs in terms of the health of the nonprofit sector.

How does the nonprofit segments' share in the Nashville MSA compare with its peers? The health care segment is strong across all MSAs except Charlotte. Nashville and Raleigh distinguish themselves from the group in terms of their nonprofits' composition: both MSAs have strong health care and education segments. Among all of the MSAs, Charlotte is visibly stronger in the human services segment.

A summary guide to the major findings and the glossary of terms used in chapter 5 are included in Figures 5.3 and 5.4, respectively.

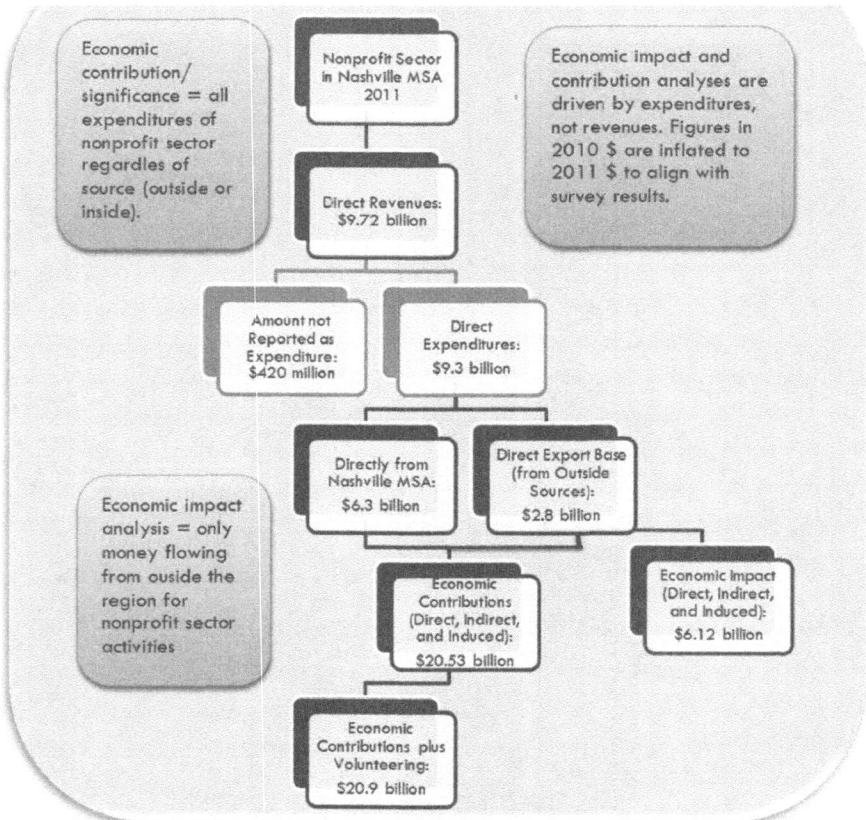

Figure 5.3 A Summary Guide to Figures in Chapter 5. *Source*: Figure created by author

Study region	The geographical area (Nashville MSA) for which economic impacts and contributions are estimated.
Nashville MSA	The Metropolitan Statistical Area including Cheatham, Dickson, Hickman, Davidson, Macon, Canon, Sumner, Smith, Robertson, Rutherford, Trousdale, Williamson, and Wilson counties.
CNM	Center for Nonprofit Management
FTE	Full time equivalency. Indicates the workload of a full time employee.
BERC	MTSU Business and Economic Research Center
IMPLAN model	An input-output modeling system. IMPLAN includes procedures for generating multipliers and estimating impacts by applying final demand changes to the model.
Nonprofit sector	Businesses that operate for purposes other than profit and are not government organizations.
Business revenue	Revenue generated from the operation of nonprofit organizations.
Impact analysis	Net new economic activity generated by the nonprofit sector, which includes the impact of dollars from outside the study region on the regional economy.
Contribution / significance analysis	Importance of the nonprofit sector to the study region: Total spending of the nonprofit sector in the local economy.
Nonprofit organization	Organizations in our study are those classified as 501(c)(3), 501(c)(4), and 501(c)(6), excluding churches
Employment	Total nonfarm employment: The number of people working for wages in non-farming related industries.
Diversity index	A summary measure that takes into account how many different types of nonprofit segments are in the dataset, as well as the relative strength of each segment with respect to number of businesses, total revenues, and total expenditures. The index becomes "zero" when there is only one nonprofit segment (i.e., human services). This study uses the Shannon-Weaver diversity index.
Export base	Net new dollars flowing into the region because of the activities of nonprofit organizations.
Nonprofit segments	There are nine major categories of nonprofit organizations used in this study. They are human services; education; health; arts, culture and humanities; environment; international; mutual benefit; public and social benefit; and unknown.
Wages and salaries (Labor Income)	Wages and salaries paid to employees of nonprofit organizations.
Direct effect	Changes in economic activity during first round of spending.
Indirect effect	Changes in sales, income or employment within the region in backward linked industries supplying goods and services to nonprofit organizations.
Induced effect	Increases in sales within the region from employee spending earned in the nonprofit sector and supporting industries. For example, doctors in a nonprofit hospital spend their earnings on goods and services in the regional economy. This spending generates business revenues, employment, and wages and salaries throughout the study area economy.
Total effect	Sum of direct, indirect, and induced effects.
Additive (Volunteering)	Estimated contributions of volunteer activities are added to total contributions of the nonprofit sector.
Enabler (Volunteering)	A component of the nonprofit sector's contributions that may have not been possible without the volunteers.

Figure 5.4 Glossary of Terms Used in Chapter 5. *Source:* Figure created by author

Chapter 6

The Northwest Tennessee Regional Port of Cates Landing

An Economic Analysis

INTRODUCTION

Located in northwest Tennessee, the proposed infrastructural development of the Port of Cates Landing will alter economic dynamics in the three-county region (Dyer, Lake, and Obion). The three counties have long been affected by the flight of manufacturing companies. Currently, both the three-county region overall and the individual counties can be designated as economically depressed areas given the fact that their (1) historical unemployment rate has been higher than the U.S. average, (2) annual average population growth rate is zero or below, (3) per capita personal income is significantly lower than the U.S. average, and (4) the manufacturing base has significantly eroded over the past decade.

The proposed infrastructure investment of $20 million in the Port of Cates Landing will create a truly intermodal transportation system in the region connecting area businesses to the Mississippi River and local and interstate highway systems (including the future I-69).

The BERC at Middle Tennessee State University has been retained by the Northwest Tennessee Regional Port Authority to assess the contributions of the proposed investment in the Port of Cates Landing to the economy of the three-county region and its surrounding areas.

Study Area

The study area in this analysis consists of three counties in the northwest corner of Tennessee: Dyer, Lake, and Obion. Throughout this study, the following phrases are used interchangeably to denote the region: Three-County

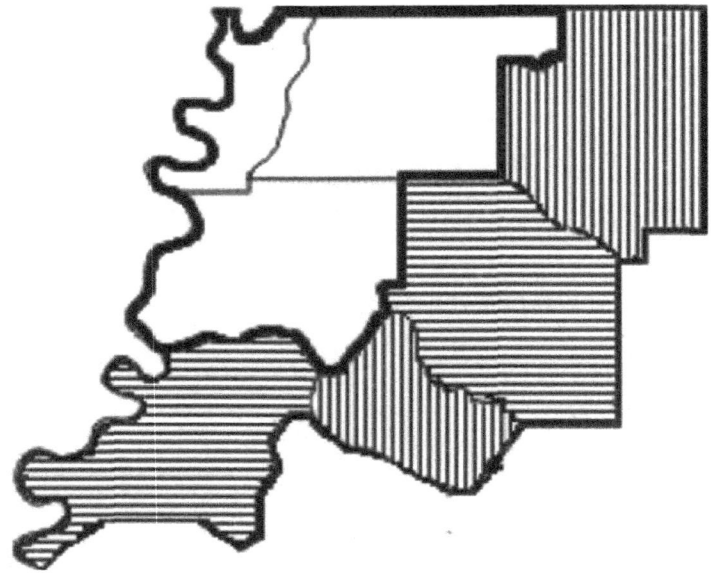

Figure 6.1 Core and Surrounding Region. *Source*: Figure created by author

Region, Study Region, Core Study Area, Core Study Region, and Core Region.

These counties are labeled as "Core and Surrounding Region" in Figure 6.1. This study often refers to the "surrounding area," "immediate neighbors," or "surrounding region" interchangeably. The shaded area, or "Immediate Neighbors," in Figure 6.1 represents the counties (Crockett, Gibson, Lauderdale, and Weakley) within a 50-mile radius of the Port of Cates Landing.

PROJECT BACKGROUND: NWTRP AT CATES LANDING

History

Established in 2001 and jointly sponsored by Dyer, Lake, and Obion counties, the Northwest Tennessee Regional Port Authority (hereafter NWTRP) is a public, nonprofit corporation whose purpose is to construct and operate a Mississippi River port at Cates Landing in northern Lake County. Given the socioeconomic challenges northwest Tennessee counties have faced since the early 1990s, there have been numerous efforts by regional stakeholders to construct an intermodal port at Cates Landing. The terrain is particularly suitable for this purpose as Cates Landing, and the proposed adjacent industrial park are above the 100-year floodplain allowing uninterrupted maritime services for area businesses.

These 20-year efforts have partially come to fruition as the NWTRP, local stakeholders, and state and federal funding partners have spent nearly $15 million to complete engineering, planning, environmental permitting and compliance, site acquisition, and harbor construction. Phase I of the Port was completed by the Army Corps of Engineers in December 2009.

At various stages of Phase I of the port's construction, several studies were conducted indicating that, once completed, Cates Landing would have a measurable effect on regional socioeconomic dynamics. The following studies highlight the critical role an intermodal port at Cates Landing would play in the region's economic competitiveness.

1. *Northwest Tennessee Regional Harbor* (2004) by U.S. Army Corps Engineers
2. *Cates Landing Port Economic Impact Analysis* (2004) by Younger Associates
3. *A Review of Proposed State Funding of the Northwest Tennessee Regional Port and Industrial Park* (2004) by Jeff Wallace and Richard D. Evans

A study completed as recently as June 2009 by IHS Global Insights, Wilbur Smith Associates, and the University of Memphis, *The Memphis Regional Infrastructure Plan*, cited Cates Landing among the top five of 25 infrastructure recommendations. The purpose of this section is not to repeat the findings of these studies but to highlight their common conclusion: if built, an intermodal port at Cates Landing would make the highly distressed counties of northwest Tennessee economically viable in the face of increasing global economic competitiveness.

Proposed Investment

As summarized above, Cates Landing is ready for a complete build-out. Incorporating an open cell design, Cates Landing would use the latest innovative strategies to create a clean (conforming to Clean Ports USA guidelines) and operationally efficient intermodal port. Meanwhile, the proposed $20-million investment to complete Phase II of Cates Landing has the potential to touch many lives in this economically distressed corner of Tennessee. A review of the letters of interest sent to the Port Authority over the past ten years suggests that the region has lost significant investment opportunities because of the lack of transportation infrastructure.

STUDY GOALS AND RESEARCH QUESTIONS

This study has five major goals:

1. To provide a brief assessment of socioeconomic conditions in the three-county region (Dyer, Lake, and Obion) from a comparative perspective
2. To provide an assessment of public benefits of the proposed investment in Cates Landing
3. To describe and analyze the short-term economic impact of construction spending related to the proposed infrastructure investment in the Port of Cates Landing, including but not limited to basic and enhanced site development and infrastructure, terminal dock site development and infrastructure, harbor and navigation lighting, and energy-efficient "green" technology
4. To describe and analyze the long-term economic impact of the proposed development of the Port of Cates Landing on the region's economy and
5. To provide a brief assessment of the implications of the port investment for socioeconomic dynamics in the region.

In line with these five goals, this study seeks answers to the following major questions:

1. What are the indicators of economic distress, and how is the study region faring compared to the U.S.?
2. Do public benefits from the port justify the $20-million investment?
3. What are the regional impacts of the Port of Cates Landing?
4. What are the implications of the Port of Cates Landing for the indicators of socioeconomic distress?

The rest of this study is organized as follows. The second section briefly introduces the indicators of socioeconomic distress in the region, highlighting primarily employment and unemployment, population growth, income, and poverty. The third section deals with the conceptual framework, study assumptions, and data. The fourth section provides the study findings organized along three major themes: (1) long-term outcomes and benefit-cost analysis, (2) job creation and economic stimulus, and (3) related jobs. The fifth section looks at the implications of the proposed investment for indicators of socioeconomic distress.

STUDY REGION AT A GLANCE: INDICATORS OF SOCIOECONOMIC DISTRESS

The counties in northwest Tennessee have undergone significant socioeconomic transformation over the past two decades: manufacturing jobs started gradually moving out of the study region, and outmigration followed. A review of commonly used socioeconomic indicators suggests that the study region and its surrounding counties are in economic distress. To illustrate the extent of the distress, this section deals with the following socioeconomic indicators: unemployment, population growth, per capita income, and poverty.

Study Region's General Characteristics

The counties in the study region are rural. This classification is based on the Census Bureau's criteria as each of these counties had populations less than 50,000 in 2009: Lake (7,303), Dyer (37,811), Obion (31,431), Crockett (14,492), Gibson (49,468), Lauderdale (26,471), and Weakley (33,459). An urbanized area is defined by the Census Bureau as "a continuously built-up area with a population of 50,000 or more." The Census Bureau also states, "Territory, population, and housing units that the Census Bureau does not classify as urban are classified as rural."

All affected counties in the study region are designated as economically distressed areas. The counties qualify for economically distressed area designation on both unemployment rate and per capita income grounds.

Employment and Unemployment

The latest available data from the Bureau of Labor Statistics on labor force, employment, and unemployment show significant differences than the U.S. average. Compared to the U.S., all the counties in the core and surrounding region have an unemployment rate substantially higher than the U.S. average. The difference in unemployment rate between the area counties and the U.S. runs as high as 6 percentage points in Lauderdale County. At the regional level, the unemployment rate is 2 percentage points higher than in the U.S. In the core region, it is 4 percentage points higher than in the surrounding region. In the core and surrounding region combined, the unemployment rate is 3 percentage points higher.

Population Growth

Used alone, unemployment rates may not reflect the true state of economic health. Unemployment rates should be used along with labor force or population data to make sense of a region's socioeconomic dynamics. For example, the unemployment rate in Lake County, where Cates Landing is located, is moderately higher than the U.S. average (1 percentage point). The primary reason for the relatively smaller unemployment rate for this county may be explained by the massive outflow of the working-age population from

Table 6.1 Unemployment Rate as of May 2010

Region	Labor Force	Employment	Unemployment	Unemployment Rate (%)	Difference from the U.S. Average
U.S.	153,866,000	139,497,000	14,369,000	9.3	
Core Region	35,058	31,205	3,853	11.0	+1.7
Dyer	17,277	15,179	2,098	12.1	+2.8
Lake	2,698	2,411	287	10.6	+1.3
Obion	15,083	13,615	1,468	9.7	+0.4
Surrounding Region	53,685	46,703	6,982	13.0	+3.7
Crockett	6,577	5,769	808	12.3	+3.0
Gibson	21,339	18,459	2,880	13.5	+4.2
Lauderdale	10,076	8,491	1,585	15.7	+6.4
Weakley	15,693	13,984	1,709	10.9	+1.6
Core and Surrounding Region	88,743	77,908	10,835	12.2	+2.9

Source: Table created by author

the county in search of employment opportunities elsewhere. The extent of the population flight from the core study region between 2000 and 2009 has resulted in a moderate decrease in population size. In this period, Lake County lost more than 8 percent of its population. In contrast, the U.S. population grew by more than 9 percent in the same period (a difference of about 17 percentage points). Five out of seven counties within the core and surrounding region recorded a decrease in average population size; however, the study area as a whole lost nearly 1 percent of its population.

Income

Per capita income is another indicator commonly used as a measure of a community's economic distress. The per capita income in the study region is far below the U.S. average. For example, per capita income in Lake County is equivalent to 52 percent of U.S. per capita income. In other words, per capita income in Lake County is 48 percent less than U.S. per capita income. Overall, the core study region has an average per capita income equivalent to 76 percent of U.S. per capita income in 2008. The surrounding region does not fare any better than the core region, as per capita income is 68 percent of U.S. per capita income. For the core and surrounding regions combined, per capita income remains at 71 percent of the U.S. average.

Poverty

Perhaps the poverty rate is the most telling indicator of socioeconomic distress. Lake County has the 12th highest poverty rate among more than 3,100 counties in the United States. Per capita transfer payments reported refer to monetary transfers from the federal government that include food stamps, family assistance, and other income maintenance benefits. Supplemental Social Security benefits are not included. In the Core Region, per capita transfer payments averaged $824 compared to the U.S. average of $419. Similar findings are present in the surrounding region where per capita transfer payments average $791.

Overall, Lake County receives twice as many per capita transfer payments as the U.S. average. This is clearly not surprising given the county's poverty rate. Nearly two-fifths (38 percent) of Lake County's population is below the poverty level. The poverty rate in Lake County is 25 percentage points higher than the U.S. average in 2008. The core and surrounding study area region has 18 percent of the population below poverty level; this is five percentage points higher than the national average.

To summarize, the combined major indicators of economic distress paint the following regional picture. Once the hub of the manufacturing sector, the counties in the study region have gradually lost their competitive edge. In turn, this gradual erosion of the manufacturing base has put pressure on social dynamics leading to massive outmigration of the working-age population in search of better job opportunities. Reversing the current trend requires significant investment in infrastructure improvements that will (a) make the region more competitive and (b) attract new or retain existing businesses, thereby stabilizing socioeconomic dynamics.

Although major investment is necessary to make the study region globally competitive, it is not itself sufficient to generate large-scale intended outcomes. The nature of investment in the region matters as much as the amount. The next sections analyze an investment of $20 million to construct a truly intermodal transportation system. Once completed, the Port of Cates Landing is likely to have a profound impact across northwest Tennessee counties.

CONCEPTUAL FRAMEWORK, ASSUMPTIONS, AND DATA

Given the extent of socioeconomic distress in the study region, the proposed $20 million investment in the port is likely to positively transform regional socioeconomics. Measuring these socioeconomic contributions is challenging given the time frame of this study (May to August 2010) due to the lack of data regarding the operational phase of the port. Ideally, a survey of local businesses regarding the potential use of the port for cargo transportation is necessary to estimate the average volume of cargo the port would handle in a given year. Cargo volume data would allow us to derive marine-related employment figures. To overcome this challenge, the BERC has developed several assumptions using existing port impact studies and regional impact assessment models to calculate average marine-related employment figures in the study region. The general assumptions and issues affecting BERC's cost-benefit analysis and economic impact estimates are:

1. The estimates of total cargo volume are model driven. The IMPLAN regional model is used to extract commodity flow data for the core and surrounding region.
2. A survey of potential port users is necessary to calculate the inbound/outbound cargo volume but was not available at time of this study.
3. The time frame for grant application does not allow us to conduct a comprehensive survey.
4. Anecdotal data from the previous Army Corps of Engineers Study, the Northwest Tennessee Regional Port Authority, and a study by Younger Associates is used in making assumptions about potential port use by sector.
5. This study has two scenarios: 1. Current cargo movement (baseline), and 2. Cargo movement with the Port Authority.
6. The first scenario (current) assumes a single-modal cargo movement (rail or truck), whereas the second scenario (with the Port) assumes an intermodal cargo movement (barge to rail, barge to truck, or vice versa).

Cargo Volume and Long-Term Job Creation

In the absence of survey data, BERC has made several assumptions to derive total cargo volume systematically. Aiding our decisions were these databases, surveys, and studies:

1. IMPLANpro economic impact model (www.implan.com) for core and surrounding regions
2. U.S. Census Bureau, 2002 Commodity Flow Survey (www.census.gov)
3. BLS, CPI-U Transportation Cost Index (www.bls.gov)
4. Congressional Budget Office, The Economic Cost of Disruptions in Container Shipments, 2006, (www.cbo.gov)
5. Northwest Tennessee Regional Port Authority business plans and other official documents (www.portofcateslanding.com)
6. Freight Analysis Framework (FAF) (www.ops.fhwa.dot.gov/freight/freight_analysis/faf/index.htm) and
7. MARAD PortKit, MARAD, A. Strauss-Wieder Inc., and CUPR at Rutgers University (www.marad.dot.gov).

Based on the aforementioned data sources and studies, BERC procedure includes the following steps to calculate inbound and outbound cargo volumes the port is likely to handle.

Step 1: Extract commodity flow data by type of flow for each region from IMPLAN (www.implan.com).

Step 2: Using Commodity Price Index from the Bureau of Labor Statistics (www.bls.gov), estimate and adjust values from 2008 to 2010.

Step 3: Estimate average value per ton of commodity in rural Tennessee by using Freight Analysis Framework data from DOT.

Step 4: Foreign exports and intermediate good imports are chosen as barge-eligible cargos. These commodities are more sensitive to changes in transportation costs.

Step 5: Adjust for shipment mode and bulk cargo. According to FAF data for rural Tennessee, trucks account for 90 percent of total shipment.

Step 6: Review and establish baseline cargo volume from previous studies. A review of previous studies based on limited numbers of shippers between 2001 and 2004 shows a cargo volume ranging from 400,000 to 1 million tons.

Step 7: Estimate price elasticity of barge transportation demand. In the absence of a comprehensive shipping survey, we estimated total shift in demand for barge operation using secondary sources.

These estimates are for the freight volume currently transported by truck but are likely to shift to the port once it becomes operational.

After calculating current cargo volume by mode of transportation, BERC then used the following steps to calculate the economic impact of port operation and marine-related economic activities.

1. Identify the share of each mode of transportation in a truly intermodal transportation system similar to the one proposed at Cates Landing (truck to barge and vice versa). The trucks in the intermodal transportation system are short trucks as opposed to the long trucks in the current system. The port business plan is used to derive these estimates.
2. Use the port business plan to identify port cargo volume by cargo type (dry bulk, break bulk, and liquid).
3. Use the findings in steps 1 and 2 as inputs to MARAD PortKit. Use the national default values for cost per ton of handling cargo and Mississippi as a proxy state for Tennessee.
4. From results in step 3, extract the direct employment necessary to handle nearly 1.67 million tons of cargo volume.
5. Use direct employment figures identified in step 4 as inputs to the IMPLAN regional model to calculate indirect and induced employment as well as business revenue, value added, personal income, and government revenues.

Public Benefits and Local Impact

A truly intermodal transportation system in northwest Tennessee would have a wide range of impact on the study region. Figure 6.2 provides a detailed view of benefit categories and expected regional outcomes as a result of constructing and operating the port and adjacent industrial park.

Assumptions and Data

In calculating cost-benefit analysis and economic impact figures, BERC has developed several assumptions regarding cargo volume, marine-related employment, transportation cost savings, major industry relocation, fatality reduction, injury reduction, and related jobs. This section briefly reviews the assumptions made and the source of data.

Construction

The majority of the proposed port-related construction spending in the core region will be in terminal dock and fill ($11 million) and in port site preparation ($6 million). These figures as well as three other minor spending

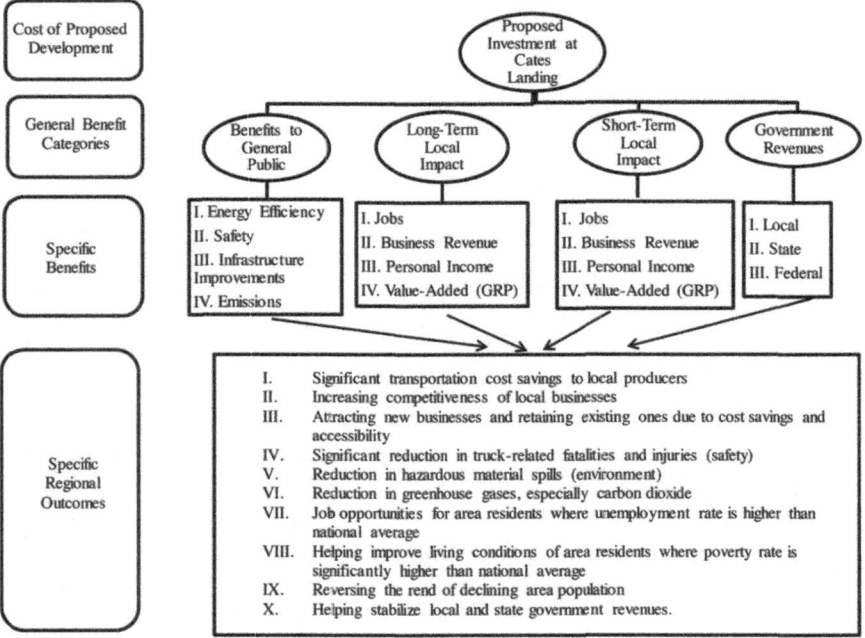

Figure 6.2 Analyzing the Benefits of the Proposed Investment in the NWTRP at Cates Landing. *Source*: Figure created by author

categories are used as inputs in the IMPLAN regional model to generate short-term employment and other regional aggregate figures. A total of $20 million will be invested in the region to complete the port's construction.

The Port of Cates Landing

The build-out scenario involving the port requires a series of assumptions regarding marine-related employment. As previously mentioned, the marine-related direct employment figures, primarily driven by total cargo volume that will flow through the port, are estimated using MARAD PortKit. The marine-related employment figures are obtained by inputting the total cargo volume information to the MARAD PortKit using national default values for the cost of handling one ton of cargo. A total of 972 direct permanent jobs will be created across more than 10 sectors in the region's economy. Major areas experiencing job creation are water transportation (366 new jobs), business services (315 new jobs), and trucking and warehousing (240 new jobs). This magnitude of job creation not only benefits area residents but also increases much-needed economic diversity in the study area counties.

Basic Cargo Assumptions and Data

Following the steps outlined in the previous sections, BERC estimated total tonnage of foreign exports suitable for barge operation for the core and surrounding regions separately. Similarly, total tonnage of intermediate goods imports was estimated.

According to BERC estimates, total Cates Landing throughput is 1,666,965 tons. Throughput includes foreign exports and intermediate goods imports, for which transportation cost saving is critically important for businesses to remain globally competitive. In 2010, the total shop of both inbound and outbound goods was for the core and surrounding region had a value of $426 million.

Consistent with the literature guiding this report, BERC forecasted cargo volume by year for the next 20 years. Port cargo volume is expected to reach

Table 6.2 Demand for Barge Transportation

	Foreign Exports		Intermediate Goods Imports		Total	
	Value	Tons	Value	Tons	Value	Tons
Core Region	$67	264,109	$244	955,245	$312	1,219,353
Surrounding Region	$23	88,239	$92	359,373	$114	447,612
Total Shipment (Inbound and Outbound)	$90	352,348	$336	1,314,617	$426	1,666,965

*Values are in Millions of 2010 dollars.
Source: Table created by author

1,843,569 by 2031, an 11 percent increase from 2012. Over the course of the next twenty years, the Port of Cates Landing is projected to reduce over 4 million ton-miles from highways, increase ton-miles for barges by more than 3 million, reduce vehicle miles of travel by nearly 15 million, and save almost 23 million gallons of fuel.

Assumptions Regarding Long-Term Outcomes

Critical for the cost-benefit analysis of the proposed investment are the long-term outcomes associated with port operation: (a) state of good repair, (b) economic competitiveness, (c) livability, (d) sustainability, and (e) safety. The assumptions and estimates regarding the long-term outcomes will be used to calculate the cost-benefit ratio. Later in this section, a summary view of calculations by the core and surrounding area businesses will be made. The calculations are based on two scenarios: the current transportation system and the intermodal transportation system.

The difference between the mode with the port and the current mode is used for all benefit types attributable to a shift in transportation from the current (single) mode to an intermodal system.

Some general assumptions are as follows:

1. We assume that current cargo volume breakdown by mode for rural Tennessee holds for the study region: 90 percent truck and 10 percent rail.
2. We assume that all trucks return 100 percent empty (load ratio of 0.5).
3. Ton-miles per gallon figures used are from a national study done by Center for Ports and Waterways, Texas Transportation Institute, College Station, Texas.
4. The Northwest Tennessee Regional Port Authority provided percentages of cargo types for the port.
5. A breakdown of the calculations are as follows:
    a. Tons = actual tons
    b. Ton-miles = tons X distance (distance to/from Cates Landing)
    c. Units = tons X tons per unit by mode
    d. Vehicle Miles Traveled (VMT) = 2 X (distance to/from X tons)
    e. Fuel (Gallons) = ton-miles/ton-miles per gallon

FINDINGS

This section presents two types of findings: (1) benefits to the general public and cost-benefit ratio and (2) job creation and economic stimulus. A few assumptions are in order:

Table 6.3 Basic Assumptions for Societal Benefits

Distance to CL (from Dyersburg and Union City): 27.5 miles
Distance to Memphis (from Dyersburg and Union City): 96.5 miles
Distance to CL (from Weakley, Gibson, Crockett, and Lauderdale): 50 miles
Distance to Memphis (from Weakley, Gibson, Crockett, and Lauderdale): 95 miles

Core Region	Tons	Ton-miles	Units	VMT	Fuel (Gallons)
Current Transportation Mode					
Truck	9,090,488	1,754,464,184	727,239	70,178,567	11,319,124
Rail	1,010,054	97,470,211	9,182		236,005
Barge	0	0	0		0
Transportation Mode with the Port					
Long Truck	7,871,135	1,519,129,055	629,691	60,765,162	9,800,833
Short Truck	1,219,353	67,064,415	97,548		432,674
Barge	1,219,353	109,741,770	685		190,524
Rail	1,010,054	97,470,211	9,182		236,005

Surrounding Region	Tons	Ton-miles	Units	VMT	Fuel (Gallons)
Current Transportation Mode					
Truck	7,833,551	1,488,374,690	626,684	59,534,988	9,602,417
Rail	870,395	82,687,525	7,913		200,212
Barge	0	0	0		0
Transportation Mode with the Port					
Long Truck	7,385,939	1,403,328,410	590,875	56,133,136	9,053,732
Short Truck	447,612	44,761,200	35,809	3,401,851	288,782
Barge	447,612	40,285,080	252		69,939
Rail	870,395	82,687,525	7,913		200,212

Source: Table created by author.

1. All dollar values are adjusted to 2010 value.
2. Life cycle of the port is 20 years.
3. Discount rates (3 percent and 7 percent) used are from TIGER II guidelines. This study also uses a discount rate of 10 percent for sensitivity analysis.
4. The value of a statistical life (VSL) and injury severity levels as a fraction of VSL are from the U.S. Department of Transportation (DOT) per TIGER II guidelines.
5. Grams of CO_2 emission per ton-mile and fatality rates, injury rate, and gallon spills per million ton-miles by mode of transportation are obtained from a study titled—A Modal Comparison of Domestic Freight

Transportation Effects on the General Public in 2007 (updated in 2009) by the Center for Ports and Waterways, Texas Transportation Institute, Texas.
6. BERC used local crash-severity data to calculate the percent of crashes by severity, and the number of injuries reduced in the study region is converted to DOT severity levels.

Long-Term Outcomes

Based on total throughput of nearly 1.67 million tons, investment in the port is estimated to generate noteworthy benefits. BERC estimates long-term public benefits for (a) state of good repair, (b) economic competitiveness, (c) livability, (d) sustainability, and (e) safety.

State of Good Repair

BERC monetized public benefits for pavement and maintenance cost savings. Once constructed, this brand new port will improve the transportation system in the region. The Port of Cates Landing is cited as one of the top five infrastructure improvements for the greater Memphis region to maintain or improve regional competitiveness. A 2010 Federal Highway Administration (FHWA) assessment of the surface transportation maintenance requirement indicates that the nation needs to spend more than $80 billion annually for highway maintenance. According to FHWA data, nearly one-third of Tennessee's highways have a Present Serviceability Rating (PSR) of less than 2.5 suggesting they are in poor condition and need maintenance.

The Port of Cates Landing would divert 1.67 million tons of cargo from long truck to short truck and barge. The resulting reduction of 141.6 million VMT would in turn create significant pavement and maintenance cost savings.

Using a conservative rate of $0.029 per VMT, BERC estimates a public benefit from pavement and maintenance cost savings of between $3 million (3 percent discount rate) and $2.2 million (7 percent discount rate) over the port's 20-year life cycle from the reduction of nearly 142 million less truck miles traveled.

Economic Competitiveness

The study region has been losing its competitive edge over the past 15 years. Job losses due to overseas outsourcing accelerated dramatically in the decade. The study region has lost 7,730 manufacturing jobs to outsourcing since 1990. The job decline in the manufacturing sector has been increasing in recent years as the study region lost 10,098 manufacturing jobs between 2001 and 2009. Unfortunately, the surrounding counties share the same fate as the core, both losing around 3,900 jobs each.

How can the study region regain its competitive position? One way is to decrease transportation costs for producers. The study region is rich in natural resources. The increasing cost of transportation is likely to put pressure on the profit margins of many manufacturing and agricultural product shippers.

Once the port of Cates Landing becomes operational, the shippers in the study region are likely to benefit from transportation cost savings. BERC estimates public benefits from transportation cost savings and indirect and induced effects on the economy.

Annual social benefits due to improving economic competitiveness over the next 10 years are expected in many areas. Over the port's 20-year life cycle, undiscounted fuel savings will be $67.7 million, and total transportation cost savings to producers will be $86.8 million. When producers invest their savings in the economy, additional jobs and income will be created. To capture this impact, BERC used the IMPLAN model for the region to estimate average annual indirect and induced value added. The cumulative 20-year value of indirect and induced value added is $12.6 million.

While these are substantial public benefits due to transportation cost savings, the port of Cates Landing would improve the region's economic competitiveness in several other ways:

1. *The study region's economy would be more diverse.* The region currently does not have a water transportation sector. Lake County, where the port is located, does not have a manufacturing sector. With the port, these two sectors would be part of the study region's and Lake County's economy.
2. The port would help retain nearly 2,300 export-dependent jobs in the study region. The steep decline in manufacturing jobs in recent years suggests that more jobs will be lost to overseas outsourcing. According to BERC estimates, nearly 2,300 jobs may be retained in the region if transportation costs decline.

To further elaborate, BERC estimated export-dependent jobs in both core and surrounding regions. The basic criterion used is that a sector must be exporting more than 20 percent of its output. The estimated port-related jobs in the core study region is 1,063. These jobs will be mostly related to grain farming (304 jobs), oilseed farming (245 jobs), and tire manufacturing (192 jobs). In the surrounding counties, Cates Landing–related jobs will total 1,230 with the majority being in cotton farming (466 jobs) and grain farming (398 jobs).

Livability

With the port, the public would benefit from reductions in congestion, accidents, and noise. Furthermore, decline in the use of environmentally hazardous materials would have important health implications. BERC monetized only societal benefits from reductions in congestion, accidents, and noise.

Average societal benefits from reduction in congestion, accidents, and noise are apparent in the study area region. Cumulative (20-year) undiscounted benefits from these three categories are estimated at around $10.6 million. Congestion ($0.048/VMT) will decrease $6.8 million, accidents ($0.026/VMT) will decrease $3.7 million, and noise ($0.001/VMT) will decrease $142 thousand.

As previously highlighted, the study area is designated as an economically distressed area with significant outmigration and poverty rates. By bringing employment opportunities to the region through the port and subsequent business expansion, the communities in the region will become more livable.

Sustainability

With the port, there would be significant reductions in greenhouse emissions. BERC monetized the impacts of reductions in the following environmentally hazardous gases:

1. VOC (Volatile Organic Components)
2. CO2 (Carbon Dioxide) CO (Carbon Monoxide)
3. CO (Carbon Monoxide)
4. PM (Particulate Matter)
5. NOx (Nitrogen Oxide)

BERC estimated societal benefits from the reduced dependency on foreign oil under "price shock value due to fuel savings." The reductions in hazardous material spills are estimated but not monetized. In all, more than 232,000 tons of hazardous materials would not be emitted. Over the next 20 years, it is projected that 230,000 tons of CO_2 will not be emitted, averaging a reduction of 12,000 tons per year.

In addition, these hazardous gases not being emitted will save over $23 million dollars. The price shock value due to fuel savings is expected to average $194,076 in savings yearly totaling a $3.9 million dollar savings.

According to BERC estimates and the Port Business Plan, the port would be economically sustainable given the volume of cargo it would handle. The revenue/income projection summary is as follows. Port and terminal operations given the initial year cargo volume of 1.67 million tons would produce revenues of $9.3 million. Total costs are expected to be $7.8 million. A net income after additional expenses is projected to be $716,139.

Safety

Following TIGER II guidelines, BERC addressed safety benefits under two categories: (1) lives saved and (2) injuries prevented. Findings show that diversion of long trucks from highways will save 19 lives and prevent 434 injuries over the next twenty years. Monetized values are estimated using TIGER II guidelines. The value of injuries prevented in 2010 dollars is valued at just over $19 million. The SVL saved, in 2010 dollars, is $114 million from 2011 to 2031.

Total Project Cost

BERC used the following cost categories to estimate the project's total cost:

1. Project cost (one time): $20 million
2. Construction labor opportunity cost: $4.2 million
3. Maintenance (dredging) and port operation (annual): $590,765

Putting aside initial and short-term labor costs, both paid for during the first year only, the yearly total cost to operate the new port would only be $590,765. In this case, the total cost includes operations and maintenance costs. Taking into account first year costs as well, over the twenty year period from 2011 to 2031, the total cost of constructing and operating the new Port of Cates Landings would be $36.6 million.

Evaluation of Cost-Benefit Indicators

According to BERC estimates,

1. Cumulative undiscounted benefits (20-year) of the port are estimated at $275 million.
2. Cumulative discounted (3 percent) benefits are $203.5 million.
3. Cumulative discounted (7 percent) benefits are $144 million.
4. As a sensitivity measure, cumulative discounted (10 percent) benefits are $115.3 million.
5. Net present value (NPV) of the port is $170 million at 3 percent discount rate; $113 million at 7 percent discount rate; and $85.5 million at 10 percent discount rate.

Benefit-Cost Ratio (BCR)

Based on the discounted benefits and costs, BCRs are:

1. 6.06 at a 3 percent discount rate, suggesting every dollar of investment will generate $6 worth of societal benefits
2. 4.64 at a 7 percent discount rate, suggesting every dollar of investment will generate $4.64 worth of societal benefits
3. 3.87 at a 10 percent discount rate

Table 6.4 Other Cumulative 20-year Benefits

Ton-Miles Reduced from Highways	4,388,554,392
Truck VMT Reduced	141,634,086
Gallons of Fuel Saved	22,832,432
Gallons of Hazardous Material Spills Prevented	15,230
Number of Lives Saved	19.01
Number of Injuries Avoided	434.52
Tons of CO_2 Eliminated	229,897
Tons of CO Eliminated	451
Tons of VOC Eliminated	33
Tons of PM Eliminated	42
Tons of NOx Eliminated	1,732

Source: Table created by author

Other Societal Benefits

Table 6.4 summarizes other societal benefits, some of which are not monetized. Notable benefits are that the port would (a) reduce fuel dependency by generating 22.8 million gallons of fuel savings and (b) prevent 15,230 gallons of hazardous material spills.

JOB CREATION AND ECONOMIC STIMULUS

Job creation and retention are critical in the study region where poverty and the unemployment rate are significantly higher than for the U.S. Furthermore, investment in the port would increase economic diversity in the region. For example, there are no manufacturing companies in Lake County, where Cates Landing is located. The port investment would attract several manufacturing companies to the area. Similarly, the region does not have any employment in water transportation. This would change with the port investment.

This section presents both short- and long-term economic impact results. To estimate short- and long-term economic impact of port construction and operation, BERC constructed a regional economic impact model (for Dyer, Lake, and Obion counties) with the widely used economic impact software IMPLANpro. Economic impact figures generated by the IMPLAN model are divided into three subgroups: direct, indirect, and induced:

1. Direct impact—involves expenditures of businesses directly related to the operation of Cates Landing.
2. Indirect Impact—involves business-to-business transactions in the regional economy triggered by the initial spending of businesses directly related to the port operation.
3. Induced impact—involves the effect of employee spending on the regional economy

In the case of Cates Landing, the short-term economic impact would look like this: the construction of the port would *directly* produce jobs in the construction sector. Then, indirect jobs would be created due to business-to-business transactions as well as induced jobs which would be produced due to the employee spending in the region. On the other hand, long-term economic impact would be a result of port operations. Jobs *directly* produced would be in marine-related sectors. Indirect jobs would come as a result of these businesses' purchases of goods and services in the local economy. Induced jobs would come as a response to the spending of these businesses' employees in the local economy.

Port Construction

Short-Run Economic Impact of the Proposed Investment

The proposed investment in the port will stimulate the regional economy by creating much-needed jobs. In the short run, construction spending of $20 million would create 234 new jobs in the region, total short-term business revenue of $26.78 million; gross regional product of $11.20 million; personal income of $8.27 million; federal taxes of $1.48 million; and local and state taxes totaling $0.49 million.

Permanent Jobs and Long-Term Impact

In the long run, the proposed investment in Cates Landing would be a boon to the regional economy. The proposed $20 million investment would create 1,700 new permanent jobs in the region. Given the nature of investment, the leverage ratio is very high: for every $20,552, one new permanent job would be created.

Considering other regional economic aggregates, the return to the proposed investment is quite handsome. For example, total business revenue (output) generated as a result of the proposed investment is $354.45 million with a business revenue/proposed investment ratio of 17.72 suggesting that for every dollar invested, $17.72 in new revenue would be generated in the region.

To summarize the findings for the long-term impact of the proposed investment in Cates Landing:

Every dollar of the proposed investment in Cates Landing would leverage:
1. $17.72 in business revenues (output)
2. $5.78 in gross regional product (value added)
3. $3.89 in personal income

Table 6.5 Job Creation and Economic Stimulus Benefits (All monetary figures are in Millions of 2010$)

Short-Term Economic Impact	Direct	Indirect & Induced	Total
Jobs	173	61	234
Business Revenue	$20.00	$6.78	$26.78
Value Added	$7.54	$3.67	$11.20
Personal Income	$6.21	$2.06	$8.27
Federal Taxes			$1.48
State & Local Taxes			$0.49
Long-Term Economic Impact	Direct	Indirect & Induced	Total
Jobs	972	728	1,700
Business Revenue	$274.97	$79.48	$354.45
Value Added	$70.85	$44.81	$115.66
Personal Income	$48.93	$28.87	$77.80
Federal Taxes			$14.18
State & Local Taxes			$7.86

Source: Table created by author

4. $0.71 in federal tax revenues
5. $0.39 in state and local revenues

In addition, every $11,765 of the proposed investment would leverage one new permanent job.

As previously mentioned, the port would likely retain much-needed export-dependent "at-risk" jobs in the region where an estimated 2,300 jobs may now be considered "at risk." Furthermore, investing transportation cost savings would create business expansion in the region, resulting in an additional 50 jobs.

IMPLICATIONS OF PROPOSED INVESTMENT FOR THE REGIONAL ECONOMY: INDICATORS OF DISTRESS REVISITED

How do the short- and long-term impacts of the proposed port investment affect the indicators of distress in the study region? This section revisits some indicators of distress presented.

Wage

In this section, we will explore of wage impact of the proposed short- and long-term investment. BERC included only direct jobs that would be

Table 6.6 Wage Impact of Proposed Short- and Long-Term Investment

	Average Wage	As a Percent of the U.S. Average Wage
Core Region		
Dyer	$30,471	66.65%
Lake	$25,721	56.26%
Obion	$35,382	77.40%
Surrounding Region		
Crockett	$31,792	69.54%
Gibson	$29,849	65.29%
Lauderdale	$29,406	64.32%
Weakley	$29,532	64.60%

Source: Table created by author

leveraged by the proposed investment in the region. Of particular concern, long-term average wages are expected to be significantly higher than the regional average. Once the port becomes operational, total payroll for permanent direct jobs is expected to be $45.5 million with an average annual wage of $46,781. In the short term, total payroll would be $4.8 million with an average annual wage of $27,556. These wages are significantly higher than average wages in Lake County where the port would be housed.

Unemployment

The impact of the proposed project on the unemployment rate is noteworthy: a reduction of 2 percentage points for the core and surrounding region and 5 percentage points for the core region. With this reduction, the unemployment rate in the core region would decrease to 6 percent and 10 percent for the core and surrounding region combined.

Poverty

The critical impact of the proposed investment will be on poverty rates in the study region (Dyer, Lake, and Obion counties). According to our estimates, the proposed development will reduce the poverty rate by one-third (5 percentage points to 12 percent) in the core region. In Lake County, where the port would be housed, we would expect a significant decline in the poverty rate from about 38 percent to at least the national average of 13 percent with the proposed investment. In addition, the core and surrounding region would have a 12 percent decline in the poverty rate bringing it down to 16 percent.

A. GENERAL ASSUMPTIONS		EXPLANATIONS
A1. The project involves diversion of long trucks to short trucks and barge		1. Current composition of commodity flows from the region involve long trucks (90%) and rail (10%).
A2. Reference area: The Port of Memphis		2. The closest port is chosen as a reference area. This provides a conservative estimate as some trucks travel from region to New Orleans.
A3. Location of the Port of Cates Landing: Town of Tiptonville		
A4. Distances		
A41. From the core region (Lake, Dyer, Obion counties) to Memphis:	96.5 Miles	3. Distance to respective regions reflects the average of distance to each county seat calculated using publicly available mapping tools.
A42. From Dyer and Obion to Cates Landing:	27.5 Miles	
A43. From Crockett, Gibson, Lauderdale, and Weakley (SR) to Memphis:	95 Miles	
A44. From the surrounding region (SR) to Cates Landing:	50 Miles	
A45. Barge operation: From Cates Landing to Memphis:	90 Miles	
B. AFFECTED REGION'S GENERAL CHARACTERISTICS		
B1. Economically Distressed Areas (all seven counties)		1. http://hepgis.fhwa.dot.gov/hepgis_v2/GeneralInfo/Map.aspx by both per capita income (BEA) and unemployment rate (BLS).
B2. Rural Areas (all seven counties)		
B3. Experiencing outmigration due to loss of jobs		
C. AFFECTED REGION'S SOCIOECONOMIC CHARACTERISTICS		
C1. Unemployment rate		1. C1 data reflects the latest available as of May 2010 from the Bureau of Labor Statistics (www.bls.gov).
C11. Core region's (Lake, Dyer, Obion counties) unemployment rate:	11.00%	
C12. Surrounding region's unemployment rate:	13.00%	2. C2 data is calculated from the Census Bureau reflecting changes between 2000 and 2009 (www.census.gov).
C13. Core and surrounding region's unemployment rate:	12.20%	
C2. Population Growth		3. C3 data is from Bureau of Economic Analysis. The latest available data for counties is 2008 (www.bea.gov).
C21. Core region:	-1.46%	
C22. Surrounding region:	-0.63%	4. C4 data is from the Census Bureau small area poverty estimates at www.census.gov. The latest estimates are for 2008.
C23. Core and surrounding regions:	-0.95%	
C3. Per capita income as percent of the U.S.		5. Lake County in the core region has the 12th highest poverty rate among 3,100 counties in the nation.
C31. Core region:	76.17%	
C32. Surrounding region:	68.39%	6. Core region includes Dyer, Lake, and Obion counties.
C33. Core and surrounding region:	71.37%	7. The Port of Cates Landing is located in Lake County.
C4. Poverty (percent of people below poverty)		8. Surrounding regions include Crockett, Gibson, Lauderdale, and Weakley counties and are within a 50-mile radius of Lake County.
C41. Core region:	17.69%	
C42. Surrounding region:	18.58%	
C43. Core and surrounding regions:	18.24%	

Figure 6.3 Port of Cates Landing: General Assumptions. *Source*: Figure created by author

D. Estimating total cargo volume for the region

Step 1: Extract commodity flow data by type of flow for each region from IMPLAN (www.implan.com)
Step 2: Using Commodity Price Index from the Bureau of Labor Statistics (www.bls.gov), estimate and adjust values from 2008 to 2010.
  Step 2.1: This process will give us the total value of commodity flows in 2010$.
  Step 2.2: Total value of commodity flows is $15.3 billion.
Step 3: Estimate average value per ton of commodity in rural Tennessee by using Freight Analysis Framework data from DOT.
  Step 3.1: Estimated value per ton in 2010$ is $811 (http://ops.fhwa.dot.gov/freight/freight_analysis/faf/).
  Step 3.2: Use average value per ton data to estimate total tons of commodity flows to the affected regions.
  Step 3.3: The affected regions account for 18.8 million tons of commodity flows.

Regions	Foreign Exports		Domestic Exports		Imports		Imports		Total Goods	
	Value (2010 Million$)	Tons	Value (2010 Million$)	Tons	Value (2010 Million$)	Tons	Value (2010 Million$)	Tons	Value (2010 Million$)	Tons
Core Region Dyer, Lake, Obion	$807	995,030	$3,144	3,877,004	$2,919	3,598,884	$1,322	1,629,624	$8,192	10,100,543
Surrounding Region Crockett, Gibson, Lauderdale, Weakley	$549	677,290	$2,404	2,964,576	$2,237	2,758,397	$1,868	2,303,682	$7,059	8,703,945
Total Shipment (Inbound & Outbound)	$1,356	1,672,320	$5,549	6,841,581	$5,156	6,357,281	$3,190	3,933,306	$15,250	18,804,488

E. Estimating Barge Eligible Cargo Volume

Step 4: Foreign exports and intermediate goods imports are chosen as barge eligible cargos. These commodities are more sensitive to changes in transportation costs (highlighted light blue columns).
Step 5: Adjust for shipment mode and bulk cargo: According to FAF data for rural Tennessee, trucks account for 90% of total shipment. Of total truck shipment, nearly 73 percent of tonnage and 23 percent of value are "bulk cargo." Since the Port of Cates Landing will handle only bulk cargo, we excluded "containerized cargo" from the analysis.
Total truck and bulk cargo adjusted commodity flows: 5.3 million tons and $1.4 billion.

Truck and Bulk Cargo Adjusted Commodity Flows

	Foreign Exports		Intermediate Goods Imports		Total	
	Value (2010 Million$)	Tons	Value (2010 Million$)	Tons	Value (2010 Million$)	Tons
Core Region Dyer, Lake, Obion	$167	653,735	$604	2,364,467	$771	3,018,201
Surrounding Region Crockett, Gibson, Lauderdale, Weakley	$114	444,979	$463	1,812,267	$577	2,257,246
Total Shipment (Inbound & Outbound)	$281	1,098,714	$1,067	4,176,734	$1,348	5,275,448

Figure 6.4 Port of Cates Landing: Cargo Volume Assumptions. *Source*: Figure created by author

F. Estimating Demand for Barge Transportation at Cates Landing (Appendix A Continued)

Step 6: Review of the previous studies based on limited numbers of shippers between 2001 and 2004 shows a cargo volume ranging from 400,000 to 1 million tons:
(1) Northwest Tennessee Regional Harbor (2004) by U.S. Army Corps Engineers, Memphis District, at http://www.mvm.usace.army.mil/environment/NW_TN_Harbor_Report.asp.
(2) Cates Landing Port Economic Impact Analysis (2004) by Younger Associates, LLC, at http://www.portofcateslanding.com/documents/Feasibility%20Study%20Younger%20Assoicates.pdf.
(3) A Review of Proposed State Funding of the Northwest Tennessee Regional Port and Industrial Park (2004) by Sparks Bureau of Business and Economic Research, University of Memphis, at http://www.portofcateslanding.com/documents/University%20of%20Memphis%20Feasibility%20Study%201.pdf.

Step 7: In the absence of a comprehensive shipping survey, we estimated total shift in demand for barge operation using secondary sources.

Step 7.1: Estimate cost per ton-mile of shipment by mode (one way): Arkansas Waterways Commission estimates

Cost per ton-mile of shipping by mode (cents)	
Truck	5.35 Arkansas Waterways Commission
Barge	0.97

Step 7.2: Estimate cost per ton of shipment from the affected regions to Memphis and calculate transportation cost savings by producers

	Cost per ton of shipment to Memphis (cents)		
	Current	with Port	Cost Savings by Producers
Core Region	516.28	240.73	-53.372
Surrounding	508.25	361.11	-28.951

With the Port of Cates Landing, producers from the core region will have 53.4 percent savings in transportation cost. The producers from the surrounding region will have about 29 percent savings in transportation cost.

Step 7.3: Estimate mode-switching rates by applying elasticity corresponding to 50 percent and 29 percent changes in transportation cost.

Mode-Switching Rates		
Change in Transportation Cost	Elasticity	Percent Change in Tonnage
50%	0.808	40.40%
30%	0.661	19.83%

Train and Wilson (2007), "Transportation Demands for the Movement of Non-Agricultural Commodities Pertinent to the Upper Mississippi and Illinois River Basin" (www.corpsnets.us).

According to a recent survey-based study by Train and Wilson (2007), a 50 percent change in transportation cost will result in a 40.4 percent shift from truck to other modes of transportation. Similarly, a 30 percent price change will result in about a 20 percent shift from truck to other modes of transportation.

Step 7.4: Apply the rates in step 7.3 to truck and bulk cargo adjusted commodity flows in step 5 to find estimated cargo volume of the Port of Cates Landing.

Demand for Barge Transportation

	Foreign Exports		Intermediate Goods Imports		Total	
	Value (2010 Million$)	Tons	Value (2010 Million$)	Tons	Value (2010 Million$)	Tons
Core Region Dyer, Lake, Obion	$67	264,109	$244	955,245	$312	1,219,353
Surrounding Region Crockett, Gibson, Lauderdale, Weakley	$23	88,239	$92	359,373	$114	447,612
Total Shipment (Inbound & Outbound)	$90	352,348	$336	1,314,617	$426	1,666,965

Total shipment through the Port of Cates Landing is expected to be 1.67 million tons, worth $426 million.

Figure 6.5 Port of Cates Landing: Cargo Volume Assumptions I. *Source*: Figure created by author

G. Total Cargo Volume and Commodity Type (Appendix A Continued)

G1. Once the Port of Cates Landing becomes operational, it is expected to handle 1.67 million tons of bulk cargo.

G2. Distribution of bulk cargo per the Port of Cates Landing Business Plan as follows:

Dry Bulk	57%
Break Bulk	40%
Liquid	3%

G3. The regions are rich in natural resources. Type of commodities to be handled are:

Major Commodity Flows by barge at the Port of Cates Landing	
Exports	Imports
Cotton	Cotton
Forestry and Logging	Forestry and Logging
Manufacturing	Manufacturing
Scraps	Mining
Grains and Oilseeds	Scraps
	Grains and Oilseeds

H. Forecasting the Growth in Cargo Volume for 20-Year Life Cycle

H1: Annual growth rate is based on annualized growth rate of cargo volume at the Tulsa Port of Catoosa in the past 20 years. Tonnage volume at this port increased 10.62 percent between 1990 and 2009 with an annual average growth rate of 0.5 percent (www.tulsaport.com).

H2: A review of studies suggests that the Mississippi Corridor has better growth potential in bulk cargo movement than other major corridors, such as East Coast, West Coast, and Great Lakes. These studies suggest an annual growth rate ranging from 0.9 to 3.3 percent. For this analysis, a lower figure of 0.5 percent is used.

H3: The following studies were consulted for the purpose of forecasting:
(a) Maritime Administration, U.S. Department of Transportation. (2008). *Impact of High Oil Prices on Freight Transportation: Modal Shift Potential in Five Corridors.* Technical Report.
(b) Regional Economic Development Center, University of Memphis. (2005). *Market Opportunity Analysis for a Short Line Railroad Connecting Brownsville and Dyersburg, Tennessee.*
(c) Younger Associates. 2001. *Cates Landing Port Economic Impact Analysis.*
(d) IHS Global Insight. 2009. *Memphis Regional Infrastructure Plan.*

H4: Over the 20-year life cycle, the Port of Cates Landing will handle 35.8 million tons of cargo.

Figure 6.6 Port of Cates Landing: Cargo Volume Assumptions II. *Source*: Figure created by author

I. Assumptions Regarding Ton-Miles and Vehicle Miles Traveled (VMT)				Explanation
I.1. We assume a load ratio of 0.5 for trucks.				Information regarding modal comparison is
I.2. Energy Efficiency				obtained from a comprehensive study by
I.21. Barge operation is nearly four times more energy-efficient than truck.				Center for Ports and Waterways, Texas
Ton-Miles per Gallon	Tons per Unit		Ton-Miles/Gallon	Transportation Institute (CPW TTI), "A Modal
Truck	25		155	Comparison of Domestic Freight
Barge	1,750 (Liquid=3935)		576	Transportation Effects on the General
Rail	110		413	Public," updated on March 2009.

I.3. First-Year Volume Snapshot—Baseline (Current) versus Alternative (with Port)						
I.31. Distance figures are from A4						
Current Transportation Mode		**A**				1. Current transportation mode is baseline
Core Region	Tons	Ton-miles	Units	VMT	Fuel (Gallons)	analysis.
Truck	9,090,488	1,754,464,184	727,239	70,178,567	11,319,124	2. Transportation mode with the Port is
Rail	1,010,054	97,470,211	9,182		236,005	alternative scenario.
Barge	0	0	0		0	3. "Tons" are the total flow of cargo to/from the affected regions.
Transportation Mode with the Port		**A1**				4. "Ton-miles" represent "tons x distance"
Core Region	Tons	Ton-miles	Units	VMT	Fuel (Gallons)	adjusted by truck-load ratio.
Long Truck	7,871,135	1,519,129,055	629,691	60,765,162	9,800,833	5. "Units" are calculated as "tons/tons per
Short Truck	1,219,353	67,064,415	97,548	2,682,577	432,674	unit" adjusted by truck-load ratio.
Barge	1,219,353	109,741,770	685		190,524	6. VMT=Vehicle Miles Traveled
Rail	1,010,054	97,470,211	9,182		236,005	7. VMT is calculated as "Units x Distance."
						8. Fuel (gallons) is estimated as
Current Transportation Mode		**B**				ton-miles / ton-miles (gallon) (I.21).
Surrounding Region	Tons	Ton-miles	Units	VMT	Fuel (Gallons)	9. (A+B)-(A1+B1) gives us VMT saved and
Truck	7,833,551	1,488,374,690	626,684	59,534,988	9,602,417	gallons of fuel saved.
Rail	870,395	82,687,525	7,913		200,212	10. Estimates for the subsequent years are
Barge	0	0	0		0	based on cargo volume forecast as explained in H.
Transportation Mode with the Port		**B1**				
Surrounding Region	Tons	Ton-miles	Units	VMT	Fuel (Gallons)	
Long Truck	7,385,939	1,403,328,410	590,875	56,133,136	9,053,732	
Short Truck	447,612	44,761,200	35,809	3,401,851	288,782	
Barge	447,612	40,285,080	252		69,939	
Rail	870,395	82,687,525	7,913		200,212	

Figure 6.7 Port of Cates Landing: Public Benefits (Assumptions and Summary Calculations). *Source*: Figure created by author

The Northwest Tennessee Regional Port of Cates Landing   135

			Explanations (Sources)
Line 1	J. First-Year Public Benefits Calculations		
Line 2	J1. Basic Parameters		
Line 3	Cargo Volume (Tons)	1,666,965	F Step 7
Line 4	Reduced Ton-Miles from Highways (Ton-Miles)	208,555,794	I3
Line 5	Increased Ton-Miles for Barge (Ton-Miles)	150,026,850	I3
Line 6	Reduced Vehicle Miles Traveled (VMT)	6,730,829	I3
Line 7	Gallons of Fuel Saved (Gallons)	1,085,058	I3
Line 9	J2. Long-Term Outcome: State of Good Repair		
Line 10	Pavement and Maintenance Savings ($0.029/VMT)	$195,194 0.029XLine 6	1. Memphis is a highly congested metropolitan area.
Line 11			
Line 12			2. Overall, there are nearly 400 miles
Line 13			of highways in Tennessee whose PSR ratings
Line 14			are less than 2.5.
Line 15			3. New port at Cates Landing will help
Line 16			relieve the pressure from highways.
Line 17			4. $0.029/VMT is estimated from DOT
Line 18			strategic plan 2010-2015.
Line 19			5. Plan calls for $85.2 billion rehabilitation
Line 20			investment for the 2.9 trillion vehicle miles
Line 21			traveled.
Line 22	J3. Long-Term Outcome: Economic Competitiveness		
Line 23	Fuel Savings ($2.966/Gallon)	$3,218,282 $2.966 X line 7	1. Energy information administration
Line 24	Transportation Cost Savings	($0.0535 X line 4/2)	(Midwest Region) (http://tonto.eia.doe.gov)
Line 25		Less ($0.0097 X line 5)	Diesel (cents per gallon) (week of August 9, 2010)
Line 26	Producers' Surplus (Indirect and Induced		2. Transportation cost savings are based on one-
Line 27	Benefits of Cost Savings)	$629,562	way truck ton-miles.
Line 28			3. Transportation cost savings are based on
Line 29			cost assumptions in F Step 71.
Line 30			4. Producers' surplus includes additional benefits
Line 31			due to transportation cost savings. We use
Line 32			IMPLAN to model indirect and induced effect.
Line 33			5. Producers' surplus includes indirect and induced
Line 34			"value added."
Line 36	J4. Long-Term Outcome: Livability		
Line 37	Social Benefits of Accident Reduction (Truck)	$0.026 X line 6	TIGER II Guidelines
Line 38	Social Benefits of Congestion Reduction (Truck)	$323,080 $0.048 X line 6	TIGER II Guidelines
Line 39	Social Benefits of Noise Reduction (Truck)	$6,731 $0.001 X line 6	TIGER II Guidelines
Line 40	J41. Not Monetized Public Benefits (Livability)		
Line 41	Tons of Volatile Organic Components Reduced (VOC)	1.57 0.02 grams X line 4	1. Grams per ton-mile for truck and barge
Line 42		Less 0.01737 X line 5	are from CPW TTI as referenced in section I.
Line 43	Tons of Carbon Dioxide (CO2) Reduced	10,925 64.96 gr. X line 4	2. CPW TTI
Line 44		Less 17.48 gr. X line 5	
Line 45	Tons of Carbon Monoxide (CO) Reduced	21.43 0.136 gr. X line 4	3. CPW TTI
Line 46		Less 0.04621 gr. X line 5	
Line 47	Tons of Particulate Matter (PM) Reduced	2.01 0.018 gr. X line 4	4. CPW TTI
Line 48		Less 0.01164 X line 5	
Line 49	Tons of Nitrogen Oxide (NOx) Reduced	82.29 0.732 gr. X line 4	5. CPW TTI
Line 50		Less 0.46907 gr. X line 5	

Figure 6.8 Port of Cates Landing: Public Benefits Assumptions and Calculations (Step by Step). *Source*: Figure created by author

Chapter 6

Line 52	J5. Long-Term Outcome: Sustainability			
Line 53	VOC Reduced		$2,035 $1,300 X line 41	1. TIGER II Guidelines
Line 54	CO2 Reduced		$229,432 $21X line 43	2. TIGER II Guidelines
Line 55	CO Reduced		$0 $0 X line 45	3. TIGER II Guidelines
Line 56	PM Reduced		$481,846 $240,000 X line 47	4. TIGER II Guidelines
Line 57	NOx Reduced		$419,678 $5,100 X line 49	5. TIGER II Guidelines
Line 58	Price Shock Value due to Fuel Savings		$184,460 $0.170 X line 7	6. TIGER II Guidelines ($0.170 per gallon)
Line 59	J51. Not Monetized Public Benefits (Sustainability)			
Line 60	Hazardous Material Spill Reduced		724 gallons 6.06 gallons X (line4/ 1,000,000) Less	6. CPW TTI
Line 61				
Line 62			3.60 gallons X (line5/	
Line 63			1,000,000)	
Line 65	J6. Long-Term Outcome: Safety			
Line 66	Lives Saved		0.9 4.351 lives X (line 4/	1. Lives saved for truck and barge
Line 67			1,000,000,000) Less	operations per 1 billion ton-miles
Line 68			0.028 lives X (line 5/	is from CPW TTI.
Line 69			1,000,000,000)	
Line 70	Lives Saved ($ SVL)		$5,419,353 line 66 X $6,000,000	2. Statistical Value of Life (SVL) is
Line 71				from TIGER II Guidelines.
Line 72				3. SVL range is between $3.2 and
Line 73				$8.4 million.
Line 74				4. Recommended value is $6 million.
Line 75	Injuries Prevented		20.65 99.044 injuries X (line 4/	5. Injuries per 1 billion ton-miles
Line 76			1,000,000,000) Less	for trucks and barges are from
Line 77			0.0450 injuries X (line 5/	CPW TTI.
Line 78			1,000,000,000)	6. Severity-adjusted values from
Line 79	Injuries Prevented ($)		$908,844 line 75 X severity-	TIGER II Guidelines.
Line 80			adjusted values	7. Police injury report in Shelby
Line 81				County is converted to DOT injury
Line 82	DOT severity levels			severity levels.
Line 83	Severity Fraction of VSL $ Value per injury	Shelby County, TN Injury Data		
Line 84	Minor 0.002 $12,000	Year	Possible injury	Non Incapacitation Incapacitation
Line 85	Moderate 0.0155 $93,000	Average (2005-08)	8084.75	3203.5 882.5
Line 86	Serious 0.0575 $345,000	Percent	0.664277058	0.26321 0.072509911
Line 87	Severe 0.1875 $1,125,000	Minor	0.5992	0.222 0.042
Line 88	Critical 0.7625 $4,575,000	Moderate	0.055	0.0312 0.016
Line 89	Fatal 1 $6,000,000	Serious	0.0095	0.009 0.011
Line 90		Severe		0.002 0.003
Line 91		Critical		0.0013
Line 92		Fatal		0.0004
Line 94	K. Job Creation and Economic Stimulus			
Line 95	K1. Construction Spending			
Line 96	Short-term construction spending impact ($)		$20,000,000	1. IMPLAN regional model for
Line 97	Short-term jobs			the core region (Dyer, Lake, and
Line 98	Direct		173 jobs	Obion counties) is used to
Line 99	Indirect & induced		61 jobs	calculate direct, indirect, and
Line 100	Total		234 jobs	induced impact.
Line 101	Slightly higher than 217 jobs per TIGER II Guideline s			
Line 102	Construction Wages (as Cost)		$4,767,188	
Line 103	Construction Wages (Opportunity Cost)		$4,185,582 line 102* (1-unemployment rate)	2. Shadow wage rate of 0.878 is
Line 104				calculated as "1-unemployment rate"
Line 105				due to high unemployment rate in
Line 106				the affected regions.

Figure 6.9 Port of Cates Landing: Public Benefits Assumptions and Calculations (Step by Step) I. *Source:* Figure created by author

Line 108	K2. Port and Terminal Operation			
Line 109	Long-term permanent jobs			3. Direct jobs due to port and terminal
Line 110	Direct jobs		972 jobs	operations are calculated using
Line 111	Indirect & induced jobs		728 jobs	MARAD Report Kit by the U.S. Maritime
Line 112	Total jobs		1,700 jobs	administration using national default
Line 113				values and Mississippi as proxy state.
Line 114				4. Direct jobs represent the jobs that
Line 115	K3. Additional Jobs Due to Producers' Surplus		50 Jobs	are required to handle 1.67 million
Line 116				of cargo volume—Dry Bulk (57%), Break
Line 117	K4. Retaining Potentially "At-Risk Jobs" in the Region		2,293 jobs	Bulk (40%), and Liquid (3%)—by
Line 118	These jobs may be lost overseas given the historical losses of jobs overseas.			barges and short trucks.
Line 119	Improving economic competitiveness of the region may keep the jobs in the affected region.			5. We then used these direct jobs
Line 120				as input to the IMPLAN regional
Line 121				model to estimate indirect and
Line 122				induced jobs.
Line 123				6. Since the region does not have a
Line 124				"water transportation sector," we
Line 125				created a new sector using value-
Line 126				added ratios from the Memphis
Line 127				region.
Line 129	L. Total Project Cost			
Line 130	L1. Construction Spending (One time)		$20,000,000	1. The requested grant amount is $20,000,000.
Line 131				2. This money will be spent in 2011.
Line 132	L2. Operations and Maintenance Cost (Annual)		$590,765	3. Operations include the management of the
Line 133				Port of Cates Landing. This figure does not
Line 134				include terminal operations.
Line 135				4. Maintenance cost is annual dredging cost by
Line 136	L3. Construction Labor Cost		$4,185,582	the Army Corps of Engineers.
Line 137				5. Opportunity cost for labor is calculated as in
Line 138				line 103.

Figure 6.10 Port of Cates Landing: Public Benefits Assumptions and Calculations (Step by Step) II. *Source:* Figure created by author

Chapter 7

Economic Impact of Bonnaroo Music Festival on Coffee County

Every year since 2002, more than 80,000 people from all over the world flock to a rural Tennessee County (Coffee) to attend Bonnaroo Music Festival. Considering the fact that the number of festival attendees is at least twice as many as people living in the county, Bonnaroo Music Festival could play a potentially critical role in the county's economy.

A PROFILE OF COFFEE COUNTY AND BONNAROO

Coffee County is located in a rural area of Tennessee between Nashville and Chattanooga along Interstate 24. A look at demographic, economic, and fiscal profiles show dramatic changes in the county between 2000 and 2005, the time period spanning the arrival of the Bonnaroo festival. The population of Coffee County grew 3 percent between 2000 and 2003, and total employment increased 9 percent between 2001 and 2004. Notable increases in employment take place in wholesale trade (52 percent), food/beverage services (19 percent), and arts, entertainment and recreation (11 percent). Only gasoline stations saw a decrease in employment (20 percent).

All other tourism-related indicators saw increases in employment rates, many of them significantly higher than the rate of population increase. Likewise, retail sales in Coffee County for 2004 were $704 million, up 11 percent over 2001 sales figures. State and local sales tax figures increased 59 percent and 41 percent, respectively, between fiscal year 2001 and fiscal year 2005. Overall, Coffee County experienced increases in employment, sales, and tax revenues between 2001 and 2005.

In comparing Coffee County numbers with the same economic indicators for the state of Tennessee, a pattern emerges. While population growth for both Coffee County and Tennessee was similar (3 percent), growth in employment, sales, and tax revenues was much greater for Coffee County than for the state as a whole. For example, wholesale trade employment in Coffee County increased 52 percent between 2001 and 2004, while wholesale trade for the state of Tennessee during that period increased less than 1 percent. Other tourism-related indicators such as accommodation, food and beverage stores, and miscellaneous retailers actually increased in Coffee County, while statewide numbers decreased.

Most notable is the gap in tax revenues. Coffee County saw an increase in state sales tax of 59 percent between fiscal year 2001 and fiscal year 2004, while the state saw an increase of only 33 percent during the same period. Similarly, local sales tax revenues in Coffee County increased 41 percent, while statewide the average increase was just 16 percent. Such a pattern of growth over the time period spanning the arrival of Bonnaroo in Coffee County, paired with the disparity between county figures and state figures, suggests that the Bonnaroo Music Festival has clearly played a role in the economic development of Coffee County.

In addition to these tangible benefits, Coffee County has also reaped intangible benefits of hosting Bonnaroo. The festival brings instant fame and name recognition to the small rural community. Young music lovers from all over the U.S. know Manchester and Coffee County as the hip place to be each June. As *Business Tennessee* notes, "After only three years, the festival has put the city of Manchester, Coffee County, and indeed the state of Tennessee on the pop culture map."

STUDY ASSUMPTIONS AND METHOD

The purpose of this study is twofold:

1. to identify economic and fiscal impact of the festival on the county's economy through visitor expenditure survey and
2. to identify the contribution of the Bonnaroo Music Festival on the county's economy through secondary data analysis.

How did BERC calculate the economic impact?

1. This study utilized survey-based estimates of total attendee spending in Coffee County.
2. In addition, festival organizers spend a substantial amount of money to prepare the campground for the festival. This data is also supplied to us by the organizers.

3. We then calculated net new spending in Coffee County.
4. Using figures for Coffee County, we calculated economic and fiscal impact of the Bonnaroo Music Festival on Coffee County using the IMPLAN software.

The Business Economic Research Center conducted a survey of more than 1,000 festival attendees to determine spending patterns inside and outside the festival area. In order to insure a random sampling of Bonnaroo visitors, the survey was conducted over all three days of the festival from two different stations on the festival site. Each day, BERC staff moved the stations to different site locations for a total of six different areas surveyed on the 500-acre site. As an incentive in soliciting survey participants, BERC staff handed out much-coveted Bonnaroo stickers in exchange for completed surveys. The response was overwhelming, and survey sites encountered long lines of participants willing to fill out the survey. BERC staff began conducting surveys at around noon each day of the festival when visitors were just beginning to arrive. In all, one supervisor and five staff members conducted 1,096 surveys, of which just 10 were incomplete or unusable.

The number of surveys conducted was determined based on ticket sales for previous festivals as well as the 2005 festival, and the margin of error is +/− 3 percent. Festival organizers provided data regarding temporary local employees, local vendors, performers and staff, and organizer spending on the festival.

Bonnaroo Spending in Coffee County

Bonnaroo festival organizers spent a total of $3.1 million in Coffee County for the 2005 festival. State sales tax on tickets accounted for $1.2 million of that total, still leaving $1.9 million spent in Coffee County by festival organizers. The largest portion of that figure went toward site-related expenditures, including rentals, preparations and site operations. In Coffee County alone, festival organizers spent $270,471 lodging the people who made Bonnaroo happen, and they spent $15,290 feeding these artists, support staff and VIPs. In addition, festival organizers paid $260,500 to local government and donated $20,000 to local charities.

Attendee Spending

In addition to direct in-county spending by festival organizers, survey responses indicate that visitors to Bonnaroo spent nearly $22 million on lodging, food, transportation, entertainment, and other souvenirs of their experience. A little over a quarter of that money, $5.8 million, was spent within the festival area on food, entertainment, and crafts.

Outside Coffee County, Bonnaroo visitors spent $7 million in surrounding Middle Tennessee counties, making up nearly one-third of Bonnaroo visitor spending. The largest spending categories were gasoline ($2.8 million) and groceries ($2.1 million).

The largest percentage of Bonnaroo visitor spending (40 percent) took place within Coffee County. Visitors spent $8.6 million in Coffee County outside festival grounds, the majority of which was spent on gasoline and groceries. Notably, visitors spent far more of their money on entertainment, artwork and crafts in Coffee County than in the surrounding Middle Tennessee counties.

In all, not including sales tax revenues, more than $11 million Bonnaroo dollars were spent in Coffee County alone.

A GENERAL VISITOR PROFILE

Who comes to Bonnaroo? A survey of 1,086 visitors during the course of the three-day festival generated the following general profile. According to survey results, visitors to the 2005 Bonnaroo Music Festival were predominantly young adults age 18 to 29.

Gender

According to survey results, more than 55 percent of visitors were male, and 44 percent were females. Males and females were almost evenly represented in the festival.

Age

Not surprisingly, an overwhelming number of attendees were young adults, age 18–29, representing 84 percent of the festival attendees. Thirteen percent were adults, age 30–44, and three percent were age 45–64.

Are they Traveling Alone?

Bonnaroo visitors tended to travel in small groups. About half of the respondents, 52 percent, came to the festival in groups of 2–4, and another 22 percent arrived in groups of 5–7. Nearly 16 percent of respondents came alone. The remaining 111 respondents came in a group larger than 8.

Where did they come from?

The survey found that Bonnaroo visitors came from all over the map in 2005. Almost all 50 states and the District of Columbia as well as Canada and a number of countries in Europe and Asia were represented in the survey individuals. Not surprisingly, the largest percentage of visitors hailed from Tennessee, but less than 1 percent of respondents originated in Coffee County. Other largely represented home states were Ohio, Virginia, New York, and Georgia. More than 92 percent of total attendees came from twenty-six states, Canada, and overseas.

Newcomers?

Bonnaroo visitors in 2005 were also, for the most part, newcomers. The majority of respondents, 72 percent, had not attended the Bonnaroo festival the previous year.

Traveling to Coffee County

In traveling to Bonnaroo, the large majority of respondents 92 percent arrived via their own vehicles. Nearly 5 percent traveled by air, and 1 percent by bus. However, many visitors used more than one mode of transportation to reach the festival.

Where did they stay?

In the communal spirit of the festival, a large majority of Bonnaroo survey respondents (89 percent) camped on festival grounds in tents or recreational vehicles. The next most popular place for visitors to stay was with family and friends, commuting to and from the festival each day (5 percent). Other visitors stayed in hotels or motels in Coffee County (2 percent) and surrounding counties in Tennessee (3 percent).

How long did they stay?

Bonnaroo visitors seemed committed to experiencing the entire festival. More than half of survey respondents indicated that they planned to spend four or more days at the three-day festival, and nearly all, a remarkable 99 percent, of the respondents planned to stay at least three days at Bonnaroo.

Where did they eat?

About 36 percent of attendees indicated that they brought their own food, 11 percent purchased from the on-site vendors, and 9 percent purchased from off-site vendors. However, a substantial number of individuals indicated that they used multiple venues to purchase food: 24 percent own food and on-site vendors, 13 percent all venues, 4 percent off-site vendors and own food, and 3 percent both off- and on-site vendors.

In short, Bonnaroo 2005 attracted young adults from all over the country and beyond to road trip with a few friends to Coffee County and camp out for the entire weekend festival patronizing a diverse group of vendors across Middle Tennessee.

CONCEPTUAL FRAMEWORK FOR ECONOMIC IMPACT ANALYSIS

This study uses the IMPLAN Model developed by the Minnesota Implan Group, Inc. to generate economic impact figures and thus to assess the effect of Bonnaroo on the regional economy. Figure 7.1 presents the Bonnaroo impact categories.

At the aggregate level, there were two sources of spending related to the Bonnaroo Music Festival 2005: festival organizers, and festival attendees. While a substantial amount of money was spent across Middle Tennessee and on the festival campsite, only the amount spent in Coffee County, excluding spending on festival grounds, was net new to the local economy. This study focuses on the areas highlighted, net new contributions that affect Coffee County.

ECONOMIC AND FISCAL IMPACT OF BONNAROO MUSIC FESTIVAL

Economic Impact

This study analyzes the economic impact of the 2005 Bonnaroo Music Festival on the local economy. Bonnaroo-related expenditures in 2005 totaled

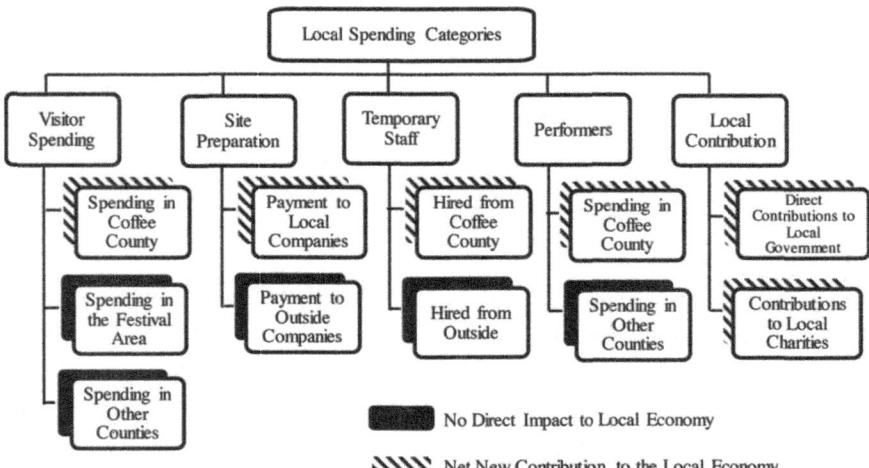

Figure 7.1 Economic Impact Categories. *Source:* Figure created by author

$10.5 million. This figure includes both visitor spending and organization spending on site preparation, rent, and spending in Coffee County by performers and staff during the festival. In addition, when money is spent in the local economy, it affects suppliers of goods and services to the local businesses. This ripple effect, or indirect impact, involves business-to-business transactions in the local economy. Furthermore, a portion of local spending by attendees and festival organizers contributes to salaries, wages, and other income for many individuals who in turn spend their earnings in the local economy. This additional economic impact is known as the induced impact.

Impact on Business Revenues

The direct business revenue impact on Coffee County was $10.5 million. The indirect business revenue impact of Bonnaroo 2005 totaled $1.3 million. The induced business revenue impact of Bonnaroo totaled $2.3 million. Therefore, the total economic impact for business revenue in 2005 was more than $14 million. Each dollar of Bonnaroo-related direct spending created an additional $0.34 business revenue in Coffee County.

Impact on Personal Income

Furthermore, Bonnaroo 2005 impacted personal incomes significantly. Households in Coffee County took home a total of $4.4 million due to Bonnaroo 2005. The majority of that was direct personal income generated by visitor, performer, organizers and staff spending in Coffee County. The indirect personal income impact of the festival totaled $436,525, the majority of which came from festival attendee spending. The induced personal income impact of the festival was more than $1 million. In all, Bonnaroo generated more than four million dollars in personal income. Each dollar of Bonnaroo-related personal income generated an additional $0.50 of personal income in Coffee County.

Impact on Employment

As discussed earlier, Coffee County experienced growth in employment rates in the period during which Bonnaroo has been held there. In fact, spending associated with Bonnaroo 2005 created 191 jobs across the local economy, many of which occurred in retail trade and accommodation and food services. The direct impact of the festival generated 145 new jobs, while the indirect impact resulted in 14 new jobs. The induced impact of the festival created 32 new jobs. Thus, the growth percentages noted above are not simply coincidental or due to overall growth in the county. Rather, they represent a substantial employment impact due to the Bonnaroo Music Festival.

Fiscal Impact

In addition to a substantial economic impact, local and state governments have also benefited from the Bonnaroo festival considerably. State sales tax on ticket sales and Bonnaroo-related spending in Coffee County generated an estimated $1.6 million in 2005.

Moreover, local option sales tax and non-tax fees levied by the county totaled $132,887. It is estimated that the city of Manchester gained $19,409 from its 6 percent hotel/motel occupancy tax. Furthermore, Coffee County received $260,500 in direct contributions by festival organizers. This includes vendor license fees totaling $2,500. In all, revenue for local governments is estimated at $412,796 due to Bonnaroo 2005, a significant fiscal impact for this small rural county.

SECONDARY DATA ANALYSIS

Since Bonnaroo's inception in 2002, the festival has become a signature event in the region. This study looked at the major macroeconomic demographic indicators to analyze any shift in the county's economic dynamics:

1. to compare changes in the county's macroeconomic and demographic indicators with that in Tennessee's indicators and
2. to analyze any structural break in the county's macroeconomic and demographic trends.

We used 28 socioeconomic indicators for this purpose. Three time-series methods are applied to 28 socioeconomic indicators.

1. Chronological clustering of sample years to provide a bird's-eye view of the region from a historical perspective.
2. Hierarchical clustering of sample years to determine which years align together.
3. Regime Shift method is used to calculate total shift in the socioeconomic structure in the country's economy between the pre-festival and post-festival periods.

All 28 socioeconomic indicators are normalized prior to analysis. As a measure of similarity between sample years, we use Euclidian nearest neighbor distance metric with 50 percent connectiveness intermediate linkage and various alpha levels for chronological and hierarchical clustering. For more information on chronological clustering and software used, see

1. Bell, Michael A. and Pierre Legendre. "Multicharacter Chronological Clustering in a Sequence of Fossil Sticklebacks." *Systematic Zoology* 36, no. 1 (1987): 52–61.
2. Legendre, P., S. Dallot, and L. Legendre. "Chronological Clustering with Applications to Marine and Freshwater Zoo Plankton." *American Naturalist* 125, no. 2 (1985): 257–288.
3. Brodgar Software at www.brodgar.com.

As previously stated, BERC used 28 socioeconomic indicators to create a comparative perspective of Coffee County and the state of Tennessee. These indicators can be viewed in Tables 7.1 and 7.2.

Chronological Clustering Analysis

Figure 7.3 represents a bird's-eye view of Coffee County's economy between 1995 and 2006. When viewing this figure, the reader should take into account that the analysis is based on the 28 county indicators highlighted in Tables 7.1 and 7.2. Each indicator is normalized using its standard deviation and mean. The normalized indicators are bounded between 0 and 1. The analysis here utilizes Euclidean measure of similarity with 50 percent connectedness intermediate linkage. At the general level (alpha = 0.01), data indicates a change in the economy around 2003.

Table 7.1 Comparative Perspectives on the Socioeconomic Indicators for Coffee County

	2006	Averages		Difference
	Latest Value	1995–2001	2002–2006	In Percentage
Population (Thousands)	51.63	46.77	50.28	7.52%*
Population (20–64) (Thousands)	30.44	27.02	29.44	8.96%*
Total Employment** (Thousands)	34.68	31.50	33.82	7.34%*
Total Earnings** (millions 2004$)	$1,269	$944	$1,217	28.92%*
Personal Income (millions 2004$)	$1,444	$1,134	$1,388	22.40%*
Income per Capita (2004$)	$27,968	$24,218	$27,593	13.94%*
Retail Sales per Household (2004$)	$37,021	$33,510	$35,914	7.17%
Mean Household Income (2004$)	$68,330	$61,122	$68,030	11.30%*
Total Retail Sales*** (millions 2004$)	$772.8	$614.2	$723.7	17.84%*
Labor Force (Thousands)	25.48	23.13	25.26	9.21%*
Housing Permits (Thousands)	0.52	0.13	0.32	142.05%*
Number of Establishments (Thousands)	1.24	1.10	1.21	9.47%*

*denotes a difference larger than Tennessee
**Includes TCPU, wholesale trade, retail trade, FIRE, and services employment/ earnings
***Includes general merchandise, food stores, gasoline service stations, apparel and accessories, eating and drinking places, and miscellaneous retail sales.
Source: Table created by author

Table 7.2 Comparative Perspectives on the Socioeconomic Indicators for Tennessee

	2006	Averages		Difference
	Latest Value	1995–2001	2002–2006	In Percentage
Population (Thousands)	6,038.80	5,557.33	5,900.57	6.18%
Population (20–64) (Thousands)	3,714.53	3,333.76	3,609.37	8.27%
Total Employment** (Thousands)	3,695.70	3,335.98	3,562.71	6.16%
Total Earnings** (millions 2004$)	$149,034	$112,868	$140,203	24.22%
Personal Income (millions 2004$)	$184,474	$149,688	$174,912	16.85%
Income per Capita (2004$)	$32,291	$26,361	$29,750	12.86%
Retail Sales per Household (2004$)	$32,360	$29,037	$31,332	7.90%*
Mean Household Income (2004$)	$78,741	$66,110	$73,063	10.52%
Total Retail Sales*** (millions 2004$)	$78,741	$66,110	$73,063	10.52%
Labor Force (Thousands)	2,990	2,807	2,911	3.69%
Housing Permits (Thousands)	46	35	42	20.20%
Number of Establishments (Thousands)	138	122	130	6.39%

*denotes a difference larger than Coffee County
**Includes TCPU, wholesale trade, retail trade, FIRE, and services employment/ earnings
***Includes general merchandise, food stores, gasoline service stations, apparel and accessories, eating and drinking places, and miscellaneous retail sales.
Source: Table created by author

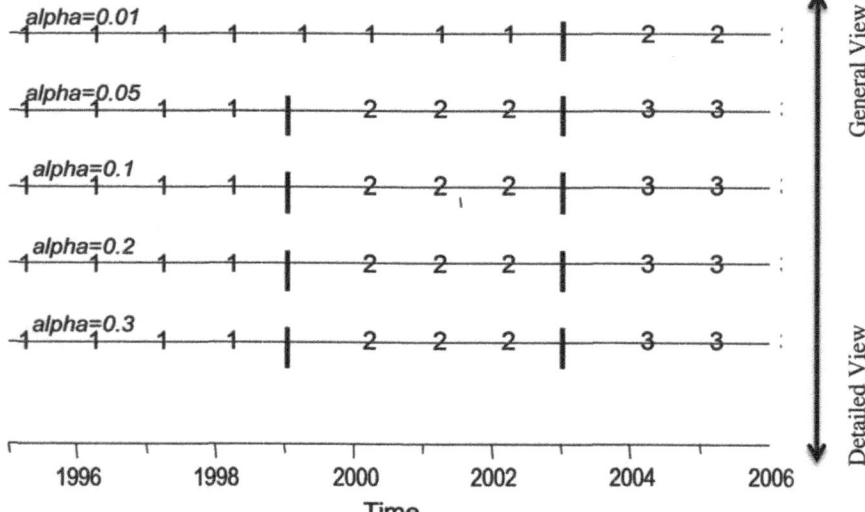

Figure 7.2 A Bird's-Eye View of Coffee County's Economy between 1995 and 2006.
Source: Figure created by author

Hierarchical Clustering Analysis

Hierarchical cluster analysis utilizes the same number of indicators (28) as in chronological cluster analysis. The analysis in Figure 7.3 provides a clear picture of how sample years are associated with each other.

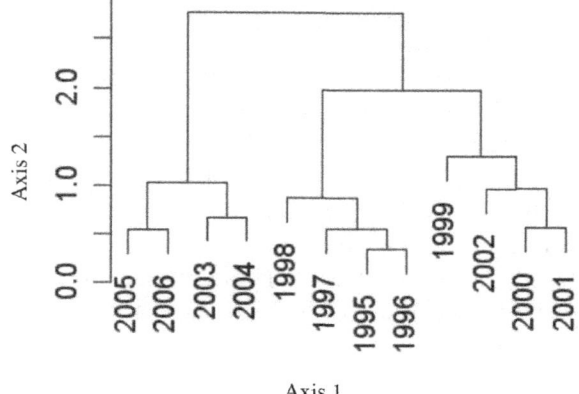

Figure 7.3 **Hierarchical Cluster Analysis.** *Source*: Figure created by author

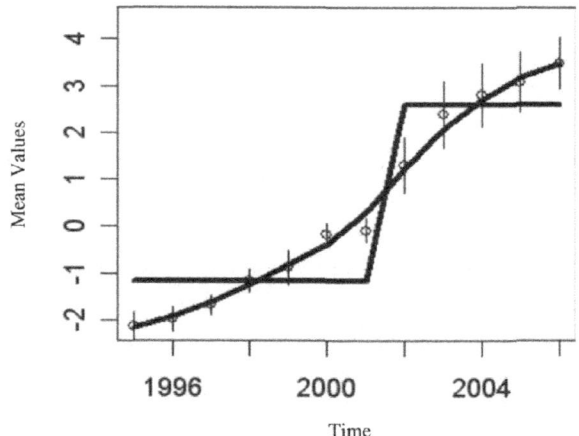

Figure 7.4 **Regime Shift Analysis.** *Source*: Figure created by author

Similarly, the years after the festival started to cluster more closely than the previous years.

Regime Shift Analysis

Regime shift analysis indicates that absolute size of the shift in Coffee County's economy between the period of 1995 to 2001 and 2002 to 2006 is 4 percent. In the same period, the absolute size of the shift in Tennessee's economy is 3 percent. Figure 7.4 represents the analysis described above.

CONCLUSION

In 2005, Bonnaroo festival organizers spent $1.9 million in Coffee County, and visitors to the festival spent $8.6 million in Coffee County for a total direct economic impact of $10.5 million. The total impact of Bonnaroo 2005 in Coffee County was $14 million in business revenue, $4.4 million in personal income, and 191 jobs. Local governments benefited a total of $412,796 from the festival. Furthermore, the quality of the festival has garnered not only praise for its organizers and performers, but also national renown for Coffee County, Tennessee. Clearly, the Bonnaroo Music Festival is economically crucial to the region.

Chapter 8

Recommendations from the Field

Addressing regional economic and business challenges requires carefully established assumptions and an in-depth assessment of the subject. Based on extensive involvement in business and economic research in both Connecticut and Tennessee, I offer the following recommendations for students of applied regional economy and strategic management.

First, any analysis of business and economic issues should start with a careful review of existing best practices in the field. Most of the time, we are not reinventing the wheel. In all cases covered in *Economic Impact or Contribution*, we carefully searched for related materials in primarily peer-reviewed journals to get a preliminary perspective on the subject.

Second, in all studies we conducted, the second step involved developing a conceptual framework to address the research questions. At this stage, all research questions, assumptions, and concepts should be identified and defined. For example, if we are analyzing the impact of an event on a region's economy, appropriate research questions, conceptual issues (i.e., impact or contribution), regional context, and survey questions should be identified, and the input-output modeling should be region-specific rather than at the national or state level.

Third, whenever possible, a survey of major stakeholders should be designed and conducted as part of the economic and fiscal assessment. The survey may achieve two things: (1) it may provide more information about the subject matter, and (2) it may confirm the major data aggregates collected from secondary sources. In all cases covered in *Economic Impact of Contribution*, we used comprehensive surveys to get a better understanding of the major issues in each of the five subject areas—health care, higher education, nonprofit sector, public infrastructure investment, and music festival.

Fourth, a business, an organization, a music event, an infrastructure investment, or an industry cluster often encompasses a lot more than a few aggregate economic or fiscal data points. It's best to gather as much information about the subject matter as time and resources allow. Gathering additional information helps one to see the big picture. Often, surveys help to accomplish this. A comprehensive survey of health care industry cluster CEOs helped us to understand major issues the health care industry is facing in the Nashville MSA. However, it is not necessary to rely only on surveys to extract information about business and community issues. For example, in the higher education study, we gathered invaluable information about higher education institutions and higher education–community interactions through surveys but also from the IPEDS database.

Fifth, whenever possible, record each step of the cost-benefit analysis or economic and fiscal assessment. Documenting the process of addressing major research questions helps us to replicate an assessment, update a previous research project, and, most important, to make the whole research process transparent. In certain cases, project sponsors may ask for annual updates. In order to maintain comparability, it is important to have a document that explains necessary procedures in order to update previous studies.

Sixth, if data and resources allow, it is important to include in the research effort a look at the issue from a comparative perspective. For example, if you are dealing with a regional-level assessment of a sector, you may include data from some peer regions. However, some impact assessments by their nature do not allow for such a perspective. In *Economic Impact or Contribution*, we were able to generate a report comparing the Nashville MSA with a set of peer regions in the health care industry, higher education, and nonprofit studies.

Last but not least, it is a necessity for researchers in applied business and economic fields to work in tandem with project sponsors without compromising the integrity of the scientific research process. Carefully developed research protocols, conceptual frameworks, research questions, and associated underlying assumptions provide necessary safeguards to ensure integrity. This process should be transparent, and sponsors should be aware of the fact that research findings may not be in line with their expectations.

I hope that *Economic Impact or Contribution* becomes a useful guidebook for students of applied regional economy and strategic management.

Bibliography

Abildgren, K. Input–Output Based Measures of Underlying Domestic Inflation: Empirical Evidence from Denmark 1903–2002. *Economic Systems Research* 19, no. 4 (2007): 409–423.

American Hospital Association. "Annual Survey Database." www.aha.org.

Andersson, Fredrik O., and David O. Renz. (2009). Building a Healthy Community Through Nonprofit Service: 2009 Annual Report on the Kansas City Nonprofit Sector. Kansas City: Midwest Center for Nonprofit Leadership.

Andersson, Fredrik O., Erin Nemenoff, and David O. Renz. (2007). Building a Healthy Community Through Nonprofit Service: 2007 Annual Report on the Kansas City Nonprofit Sector. Kansas City: Midwest Center for Nonprofit Leadership.

Andersson, Fredrik, Scott Helm, Benjamin Nemenoff, and David Renz. (2006). Building a Healthy Community Through Nonprofit Service: 2006 Annual Report on the Kansas City Nonprofit Sector. Kansas City: Midwest Center for Nonprofit Leadership.

Andrews, I. A. (1999, September). Cost-Benefit Analysis in Financial Regulation. *Financial Services Authority Occasional Paper*, 1–27.

Appleseed (2003). Engines of Economic Growth: Economic Impact of Boston's Eight Research Universities on the Metropolitan Boston Area. New York: Appleseed.

Araujo, P. Q. (2013). Productive Structure and the Functional Distribution of Income: An Application of the Input-Output Model. *CEPAL Review*, 57–78.

Arik, Murat, and Christian Nsiah. (2004). Measuring the Economic Impact of Middle Tennessee State University. Murfreesboro; Middle Tennessee State University: Business and Economic Research Center.

Armstrong, Martin, and Jim Taylor. Regional Economics and Policy, 3rd Edition. Malden: Wiley-Blackwell, 2000. "Association of University Technology Managers." www.autm.net.

Atterton, A. S. The Contribution of Rural Business to Community Resilience. *Local Economy* 29, no. 3 (2014): 228–244.

Barker, S. (2003). Counterfactual Analyses of Causation: The Problem of Effects and Epiphenomena Revisited. *Nous*, 133–150.

Barro, R. J., and Jong-Wha Lee. International Comparisons of Educational Attainment. *Journal of Monetary Economics* 32, no. 3 (1993): 363–394.

Becker's Hospital Review. http://www.beckershospitalreview.com.

Bell, Michael A. and Pierre Legendre. Multicharacter Chronological Clustering in a Sequence of Fossil Sticklebacks. *Systematic Zoology* 36, no. 1 (1987): 52–61.

Benhabib, Jess, and Mark M. Spiegel. The Role of Human Capital in Economic Development: Evidence from Aggregate Cross-Country Data. *Journal of Monetary Economics* 34 (1994): 143–173. "British Higher Educations- Business and Community Interaction Survey." www.hefce.ac.uk.

Bergman, Edward M. and Edward J. Feser (1999). Industrial and Regional Clusters: Concepts and Comparative Applications. Morgantown: West Virginia University: Regional Research Institute.

Berry, Suzanne L., and Stan Spurlock (2002). Measuring the Impact of the Healthcare Sector on a Local Economy: Sharkey-Issaquena County, Mississippi. Mississippi State: Mississippi State University.

Bimal Arora, S. B. Performing Citizenship: An Innovative Model of Financial Services for Rural Poor in India. *Business & Society* 51, no. 3 (2012): 450–477.

Bogen, J. Analysing Causality: The Opposite of Counterfactual is Factual. *International Studies in the Philosophy of Science* 18, no. 1 (2004): 3–26.

Bon, R. Comparative Stability Analysis of MultiRegional Input-Output Models: Column, Row and Leontief-Strout Gravity Coefficient Models. *The Quarterly Journal of Economics* 99, no. 4 (1984): 791–815.

Bose, A. Kolkata's Early Chinese Community and their Economic Contributions. *South Asia Research SAGE* 33, no. 2 (2013): 163–176.

Boster, Ronald S., and W. E. Martin. The Value of Primary vs. Secondary Data in Interindustry Analysis: A Study in the Economics of the Economic Models. *Arizona Agricultural Experiment Station Journal* 6, no. 2 (n.d.): 35–44.

Brannstrom, L. Poor Places, Poor Prospects? Counterfactual Models of Neighbourhood Effects on Social Exclusion in Stockholm, Sweden. *Urban Studies* 41, no. 13 (2004): 2515–2537.

Brodgar Software. www.brodgar.com.

Bureau of Economic Analysis (BEA). www.bea.gov.

Bureau of Labor Statistics (BLS). www.bls.gov.

Business Facilities. www.businessfacilities.com.

Carly A. Dean, B. D. Fath, Bin Chen. Indicators for an Expanded Business Operations Model to Evaluate. *Elsevier* 47 (2014): 137–148.

Carstensen, Fred, et al. (2001). The Second MetroHartford Regional Performance Benchmark. Storrs; Connecticut Center for Economic Analysis: University of Connecticut.

CB Richard Ellis (CBRE). www.cbre.com.

Census Bureau. "North American Industrial Classification System (NAICS)." www.census.gov/eos/www/naics.

Census Bureau. www.census.gov.

Center for Economic Development Research (2001). The Economic Contributions of Baptist Health Systems of South Florida. Tampa: University of South Florida.

Center for Medicare and Medicaid Services. www.cms.hhs.gov.

Chase, Robert A. (2002). The Biotechnology and Medical Device Industry in Washington State: An Economic Analysis. Kirkland: Huckell/Weinman Associates, Inc.

Chase, Robert A. (2004). *Economic Contribution of the Healthcare Industry to the City of Seattle*. Kirkland: Huckell/Weiman Associates.

Christophersen, Nadreau, and Olanie (January 7, 2014). The Rights and Wrongs of Economic Impact Analysis for Colleges and Universities. *Economic Modeling Specialists International (EMSI)*. Blog entry by Joshua Wright.

Coates, John C. Cost-Benefit Analysis of Financial Regulation: Case Studies and Implications. *Yale Law Journal* 124, no. 4 (2015): 882–1011.

Clower, Terry L., and Bernard L. (1998). Weinstein. The Dallas Fort Worth Healthcare Industry: Economic Impacts and Growth Potential. Denton: University of North Texas.

Coleman, James S. (1990). Foundations of Social Theory. Cambridge: Harvard University Press.

Conference Board. www.conference-board.org.

Coomes, Paul, and Raj Narang (2001). *Louisville's Health-Related Economy: Size, Character, and Growth*. Louisville: University of Louisville.

Cortés-Bordaa, D., Ruiz-Hernándeza, A., and Guillén-Gosálbez G. Identifying Strategies for Mitigating the Global Warming Impact of the Eu-25 Economy Using a Multi-Objective Input–Output Approach. *Energy Policy* 77 (2015): 21–30.

Cunningham, Lawrence F., and Moonkyu Lee. A Cost/Benefit Approach to Understanding Service Loyalty. *Journal of Services Marketing* 15, no. 2 (2001): 113–130.

Dahlsrud, A. How Corporate Social Responsibility is Defined: An Analysis of 37 Definitions. *Corporate Social Responsibility and Environmental Management* 15, no. 1 (2006): 1–13.

Daniel J. Bearupa, N. D. Evans, and M. J. Chappell. The Input–Output Relationship Approach to Structural Identifiability Analysis. *Computer Methods and Programs in Biomedicine* 109, no. 2 (2013): 171–181.

David R. Millen, M. A. Fontaine, and Michael J. Muller. Understanding the Benefits and Costs of Communities of Practice. *Communications of the ACM* 45, no. 4 (2002): 69–73.

Doeksen, Gerald A., and Val Schott (2002). The Economic Importance of the Health-Care Sector in a Rural Economy. Stillwater: Oklahoma State University.

Doh, J. A. The High Impact of Collaborative Social Intitiatives. *MIT Sloan Management Review* (2005): 30–39.

Doyle, Christopher, and Martin Weale. Education, Externalities, Fertility, and Economic Growth. *Education Economics* 2, no. 2 (1994): 129–168.

Engage Consulting Limited (2010). *ENA High Level Smart Metering Cost Benefit Analysis*.

Evans, Garen K. (2004). East Central Mississippi Health Network: Economic Impact Analysis. Mississippi State: Mississippi State University.

Expansion Management. http://www.expansionmanagement.com.

Ferng, J.-J. Applying Input–Output Analysis to Scenario Analysis of Ecological Footprints. *Ecological Economics* 69, no. 2 (2009):345–354.

Florida, Richard. (2005). Cities and the Creative Class. New York: Routledge.

Garmise, Shari (2006). People and the Competitive Advantage of Place: Building a Workforce for the 21st Century. New York: M.E. Sharp.

Glasson, John. The Widening Local and Regional Development Impact of the Modern Universities: A Tale of Two Cities and North-South Perspectives. *Local Economy* 2, no. 2 (2003): 21–37.

Goldstein, Harvey, and Joshua Drucker. The Economic Development Impacts of Universities on Regions: Do Size and Distance Matter? *Economic Development Quarterly* 20, no. 1 (2006): 22–43.

Goldstein, Harvey, Michael Luger, and Gunther Maier. (1995). The University as an Instrument for Economic and Business Development: U.S. and European Comparisons." In Emerging Patterns of Social Demand and University Reform: Through a Glass Darkly by David D. Dill and Barbara Sporn, 105–133. Oxford: Pergamon.

Gregory Kelly, Andrew Cooper, and Evelyn Pinkerton. Social Network Analysis, Markov Chains and Input-Output Models: Combining Tools to Map and Measure the Circulation of Currency in Small Economies. *Journal of Rural and Community Development* 9, no. 3 (2014): 118–141.

Groot, Wim and Hessel Oosterbeek. Earnings Effects of Different Schoolings; Human Capital Versus Screening. *The Review of Economics and Statistics* 76, no. 2 (1994): 317–321.

Hall, N. Non-locality on the Cheap? A New Problem for Counterfactual Analyses of Causation. *Nous* 36, no. 2 (2002): 276–294.

Harris, H. Content Analysis of Secondary Data: A Study of Courage in Managerial Decision Making. *Journal of Business Ethics* 34 (2001): 191–208.

Harris, Thomas et al. Economic Impact and Linkages of the Local Health Sector on the Economy of Lander County, Nevada, 2000. Reno: University of Nevada, Reno; 2004.

Heene, J. L. Investigating the Impact of Firm Size on Small Business Social Responsibility: A Critical Review. *Journal of Business Ethics* 67, no. 3 (2006): 257–273.

Heinzerling, F. A. (2002). Pricing the Priceless: Cost-Benefit Analysis of Environmental Protection. *University of Pennsylvania Law Review* 1553–1584.

Helm, Scott, Ben Nemenoff, and David O. Renz (2005). Building a Healthy Community Through Nonprofit Service: 2005 Annual Report on the Kansas City Nonprofit Sector. Kansas City: Midwest Center for Nonprofit Leadership.

Higgins, Scott E., and Kristy Karl (2003). Measuring the Impact of the Healthcare Sector on Swain County, North Carolina. Cullowhee: Western Carolina University.

Hofferth, S. L. Secondary Data Analysis in Family Research. *Journal of Marriage and Family* 67, no. 4 (2005): 891–905.

Iftikhar Alam, Shah Khusro, Azhar Rauf, Qamruz Zaman. Conducting Surveys and Data Collection: From Traditional to Mobile and SMS-based Surveys. *Pakistan Journal of Statistics and Operation Research* 10, no. 2 (2014): 169–187.

IHS Global Insights, Wilbur Smith Associates, and The University of Memphis (2009). The Memphis Regional Plan. Memphis: HIS Global Insights, Wilbur Smith Associates, and the University of Memphis.

IMPLANpro Inc. www.implan.com.

Ivo Zander, P. M.-Covin, and Elizabeth L. Rose. Born Globals and International Business: Evolution of a Field of Research. *Journal of International Business Studies*, 46 (2015): 27–35.

Jaya Prasad Tripathy. Secondary Data Analysis: Ethical Issues and Challenges. *Iranian Journal of Public Health* 42, no. 12 (2013): 1478–1479.

Jenkins, Steve, and Jon Pratt (2010). Nonprofit Current Conditions Report: Analysis of a Minnesota Council of Nonprofit Member Survey. Saint Paul: Minnesota Council of Nonprofits.

Juan Alvarez, J. C. Knowledge Creation and the Use of Secondary Data. *Journal of Clinical Nursing*, 21, no. 19–20 (2012): 2699–2710.

Kakoli Borkotoky, S. U. (2014). Indicators to Examine Quality of Large Scale Survey Data: An Example through District Level Household and Facility Survey. *PLOS ONE*, 1–12.

Kentucky Nonprofit Network (2012). More than Charity Kentucky's Nonprofit Sector. Lexington: Kentucky Nonprofit Network.

Kleinrichert, Denise, Jennifer Tosti-Kharas, Michael Albert, and Jamie P. Eng. The Effect of a Business and Society Course on Business Student Attitudes Toward Corporate Social Responsibility. *Journal of Education for Business* 88, no. 4 (2013): 230–237.

Klier, Thomas, and William Testa (2002). Location Trends of Large Company Headquarters During the 1990s. Economic Perspectives. Chicago: Federal Reserve Bank of Chicago.

Kobeissi, N. Impact of the Community Reinvestment Act on New Business Start-Ups and Economic Growth in Local Markets280. *Journal of Small Business Management* 47, no. 4 (2009): 489–513.

Kozmetsky, George, Frederick Williams, and Victoria Williams (2004). New Wealth: Commercialization of Science and Technology for Business and Economic Development. Westport: Praeger.

Krueger, Alan B., and Mikael Lindahl. Education for Growth: Why and for Whom? *Journal of Economic Literature* 39 (2001): 1101–1136.

Larry H. P. Lang, R. M. Stulz. Tobin's q, Corporate Diversification, and Firm Performance. *Journal of Political Economics* 102, no. 6 (1994): 1248–1280.

Lazarus, William F., and David A. Nelson (2002). Renville County: Economic Impact of the Healthcare Sector. Minneapolis; University of Minnesota.

Legendre, P., S. Dallot, and L. Legendre. Chronological Clustering with Applications to Marine and Freshwater Zoo Plankton. *American Naturalist* 125, no.2 (1985): 257–288.

Leonardo Caggiani, M. O. Handling Uncertainty in Multi Regional Input-Output Models by Entropy Maximization and Fuzzy Programming. *Transportation Research Part E: Logistics and Transportation Review* 72 (2014): 159–172.

LexisNexis Academic Universe. www.lexisnexis.com.

Littlepage, Mary Kress 2010. State of the Sector. Jacksonville: Nonprofit Center of Northeast Florida.

Llopa, Maria, Antonio Manresa (2014). Comparing the Aggregation Bias in the Input-Output model and the Social Accounting Matrix Model. *Applied Economics Letters* 21, no. 11 (2014): 795–800.

Lucas, Robert E., Jr. On the Mechanics of Development. *Journal of Monetary Economics* 22 (1988): 3–42.

Maine Association of Nonprofits (2010). Partners in Prosperity: The Maine Nonprofit Sector Impact. Portland: Maine Association of Nonprofits.

Maine Association of Nonprofits (2013). Partners in Prosperity: The Maine Nonprofit Sector Impact. Portland: Maine Association of Nonprofits.

Mankiw, N. Gregory, David Romer, and David N. Weil. A Contribution to the Empirics of Economic Growth. *Quarterly Journal of Economics* 107 (1992): 407–437.

MARAD Port Kit. http://www.marad.dot.gov/ports/strongports/port-planning-and-investment-toolkit.

Market Street Services, Inc. (2005). *Target Business Analysis: Nashville, TN*. Atlanta: Market Street Services.

Market Street Services, Inc. (2010). *Target Business Analysis: Nashville, TN*. Atlanta: Market Street Services.

Marroni, M. (2014). Production of Commodities by Means of Processes the Flow–Fund Model, Input–Output Relations and the Cognitive Aspects of Production. *Structural Change and Economic Dynamics* 29 (2014): 5–18.

Meng-Hsiang Hsu, Teresa L. Ju, Chia-Hui Yen, Chun-Ming Chang. Knowledge Sharing Behavior in Virtual Communities: The Relationship Between Trust, Self-Efficacy, and Outcome Expectations. *International Journal of Human Computer Studies* 65, no. 2 (2007): 153–169.

Metropolitan Chicago Healthcare Council (2004). The Economic Impact of Chicago's Hospitals on the Metropolitan Chicago Area. Chicago.

Michael L. Johnson, P. W. Good Research Practices for Comparative Effectiveness Research: Analytic Methods to Improve Causal Inference from Nonrandomized Studies of Treatment Effects Using Secondary Data Sources: The ISPOR Good Research Practices for Retrospective Database Analysis. *Value Health*, 12, no. 8 (2009): 1062–1073.

Midwest Center for Nonprofit Leadership (2009). The 2009 Missouri Nonprofit Sector at a Glance. Kansas City: Midwest Center for Nonprofit Leadership.

Mincer, Jacob (1974). Schooling, Experience, and Earnings. New York: Columbia University Press.

Montana Nonprofit Association (2007). The Montana Nonprofit Sector. Helena: Montana Nonprofit Association.

MTSU Business and Economic Research Center. www.mtsu.edu/BERC.

Nashville Chamber of Commerce. www.nashvillechamber.com.

Nashville Health Care Council (NHCC). www.healthcarecouncil.com.

National Center for Charitable Statistics (NCCS). www.nccs.urban.org.

New Hampshire Center for Nonprofits (2009). Essential: A Portrait of the Nonprofit Sector in New Hampshire. Concord: New Hampshire Center for Nonprofits.

New Hampshire Center for Nonprofits (2012). New Hampshire's Nonprofit Sector in Brief. Concord: New Hampshire Center for Nonprofits.

New Jersey Center for Non-Profits (2009). New Jersey's Non-Profit Sector: An Economic Force for Strengthening the Garden State. North Brunswick: New Jersey Center for Non-Profits.

New Jersey Center for Non-Profits (2012). New Jersey Non-Profits 2012: Trends and Outlook. North Brunswick: New Jersey Center for Non-Profits.

Neumayer, E. Do We Trust Data? On the Validity and Reliability of Cross-National Environmental Surveys. *Social Science Quarterly* 83, no. 1 (2003): 332–340.

Nieuwland, M. S. Establishing Propositional Truth-Value in Counterfactual and Real-World Contexts During Sentence Comprehension: Differential Sensitivity of the Left and Right Inferior Frontal Gyri. *Elsevier* 59, no. 4 (2012): 3433–3440.

Nimon, K. Secondary Data Analyses From Published Descriptive Statistics: Implications for Human Resource Development Theory, Research and Practice. *Advances in Developing Human Resources* 17, no. 1 (2014): 26–39.

Norsworthy, K. O. A Review of Industry Aggregation in Input Output Models. *American Economist* 20, no. 1 (1976): 5–10.

North Dakota Association of Nonprofit Organizations (2013). North Dakota's Nonprofit Sector in Brief. Bismark: North Dakota Association of Nonprofit Organizations.

North Dakota Association of Nonprofit Organizations (2011). Vibrant. Diverse. Essential. The North Dakota Nonprofit Sector. Bismark: North Dakota Association of Nonprofit Organizations.

Northwest Tennessee Regional Port Authority. www.cateslanding.com.

OCED, Centre for Educational Research and Innovation (1998). Human Capital Investment: An International Comparison. Paris: OCED Publishing.

OCED, Centre for Educational Research and Innovation (2001). The Well-Being of Nations: The Role of Human and Social Capital. Paris: OCED Publishing.

Oldakowski, Ray, and Mary Kress Littlepage (2012). State of the Sector: How Northeast Florida's Nonprofits Have Changed and Adapted in Good Times and Bad. Jacksonville: Nonprofit Center of Northeast Florida.

Omer Farooq, M. P. (n.d.). The Impact of Corporate Social Responsibility on Organizational Commitment: Exploring Multiple Mediation Mechanisms.

Otte, R. Counterfactuals and Epistemic Probability. *Synthese* 152, no. 1 (2006): 81–93.

Partnership for Michigan's Health (2005). The Economic Impact of Health Care in Michigan. Second Edition. Okemos.

Paul, L. Keeping Track of the Time: Emending the Counterfactual Analysis of Causation. *Analysis* 58, no. 3 (1998): 191–198.

Pedro Cavalvanti Ferriera, J. V. (2005). An Investigation of Cross-Country Income. *Revista de Analisis Economico* 20, no. 2 (2005): 3–21.

Perry, David C., and Wim Wiewel. (2005). The University as Urban Developer: Case Studies and Analysis. New York: M.E. Sharp.

Pesaran, R. P. (2012, June). Counterfactual Analysis in Macroeconometrics: An Empirical Investigation into the Effects of Quantitative Easing. *IZA*, 1–19.

Philadelphia Federal Reserve. www.philadelphiafed.org.

Philip Watson, J. W. Determining Economic Contributions and Impacts: What is the difference and why do we care? *The Journal of Regional Analysis & Policy*, 37, no. 2 (2007): 15–19.

Pi-Cheng Chen, Douglas Crawford-Brown, Chi-Hui Chang, and Hwong-wen Ma. Identifying the Drivers of Environmental Risk through a Model Integrating

Substance Flow and Input–Output Analysis. *Ecological Economics* 107 (2014): 94–103.

Porter, Michael (1990). The Competitive Advantage of Nations. New York: The Free Press.

Porter, Michael. Location, Competition, and Economic Development: Local Clusters in the Global Economy. *Economic Development Quarterly* 14 (2000): 15–34.

Prasad, J. Secondary Data Analysis: Ethical Issues and Challenges. *Iranian Journal of Public Health* 42, no. 12 (2013): 1478–1479.

PricewaterhouseCoopers. Venture Economics/National Venture Capital Association Money Tree Survey. www.pwcmoneytree.com.

Putnam, Robert D. (1993). Making Democracy Work: Civic Traditions in Modern Italy. Princeton: Princeton University Press.

R. Kerry Turner, et al. Ecological-economic Analysis of Wetlands: Scientific Integration for Management and Policy. *Ecological Economics* 35, no. 1 (2000): 7–23.

ReferenceUSA. www.referenceusa.com.

Romer, Paul M. Human Capital and Growth: Theory and Evidence. Carnegie- Rochester Conference Series on Public Policy 32, no.1 (1990): 251–286.

Romer, Paul M. Increasing Returns and Long-Run Growth. *Journal of Political Economy* 94 (1986): 1002–1037.

Saxenian, AnnaLee (1996). Regional Advantage: Culture and competition in the Silicon Valley and Route 128. Cambridge: Harvard University Press.

Schröer, Andreas, Dahnesh Medora, Anindita Mukerjee, and Greg Wallinger (2012). Oregon Nonprofit Sector Report: The State of the Nonprofit Sector in Oregon 2011. Portland: Nonprofit Association of Oregon.

Seltzer, A., and Jesper Bagger. Administrative and Survey Data in Personnel Economics. *The Australian Economic Review* 47, no. 1 (2014): 137–146.

Shabana, Kareem M., and Archie B. Carroll. The Business Case for Corporate Social Responsibility: A Review of Concepts, Research and Practice. *International Journal of Management Reviews* 12, no. 1 (2010): 85–105.

Shaffer M. L. and Chinchilli, V. M. A Likelihood-Based, Counterfactual Approach to Accounting for Treatment Failures in Clinical Trials. *Journal of Biopharmaceutical Statistics* 13, no. 3 (2003): 1054–3406.

Simon, K. E. (2001). Using Cost Benefit Analysis for Enterprise Resource Planning Project Evaluation: A Case for Including Intangibles. *34th Hawaii International Conference on System Sciences*, 1–11.

Simpson, T. K. The Link Between Corporate Social and Financial Performance: Evidence from the Banking Industry. *Journal of Business Ethics* 35, no. 2 (2002): 97–109.

Simpson, Kit N., and B. C. Tilley. Economic Analysis of Secondary Trial Data. *Elsevier—Progress in Cardiovascular Diseases* 54, no. 4 (2012): 351–356.

Smith, Adam (1991[1776]). The Wealth of Nations. New York: Alfred A. Knopf.

Spash, N. H. (1993). *Cost-Benefit Analyses and the Environment.* Massachusetts: Edward Elgar Publishing Limited.

Sperling, Bert, and Peter Sander (2007). *Cities Ranked and Rated.* Hoboken, NJ: Wiley.

Spielman, Seth E., and D. C. Folch. Reducing Uncertainty in the American Community Survey through Data-Driven Regionalization. *PLoS One* 10, no. 2 (2015): 1–21.

State Occupational Projections. www.projectionscentral.com.

Sudo, N. Sectoral Comovement, Monetary Policy Shocks, and Input–Output Structure. *Journal of Money, Credit and Banking* 44, no. 6 (2012): 1225–1244.

Sugimoto, G. D. West African Single Currency and Competitiveness. *Review of Development Economics* 17, no. 4 (2013): 763–777.

Tennessee Advisory Commission on Intergovernmental Relations (TACIR). www.state.tn.us/tacir.

Tennessee Department of Labor and Workforce Development. www.state.tn.us/labor-wfd.

Tennessee Department of Health. www.state.tn.us/health.

Thanki, Roisin. How do we Know the Value of Higher Education to Regional Development? *Regional Studies* 33, no.1 (1999): 84–89.

U.S. Army Corps of Engineers. http://www.mvm.usace.army.mil.

U.S. Army Corps of Engineers (2004). Northwest Tennessee Regional Harbor. Memphis: U.S. Army Corps of Engineers.

U.S. Department of Education. www.ed.gov.

United States of America. The Congress of the United States. Congressional Budget Office. The Economic Costs of Disruptions in Container Shipments. By Bruce Arnold, Craig Cammarata, Dick Farmer, Kim Kowaleski, Fatimot Ladipo, Mark Lasky, and David Moore. 2006.

University of Tennessee, State Data Center. cber.bus.utk.edu.

Urban Land Institute. www.uli.org.

Veleva, Vesela, et al. Measuring the Business Impacts of Community Involvement: The Case of Employee Volunteering at UL. *Business and Society Review* 117, no. 1 (2012): 123–142.

Vermont Community Foundation (2011). Vermont's Nonprofit Sector: A Vita Community in a Time of Change. Middlebury: Vermont Community Foundation.

Wallace, Jeff, and Richard D. Evans (2004). A Review of Proposed State Funding of the Northwest Tennessee Regional Port and Industrial Park. Memphis: Sparks Bureau of Business and Economic Research.

Wang, Samuel J., et al. A Cost-benefit Analysis of Electronic Medical Records in Primary Care. *The American Journal of Medicine*, 114, no. 5 (2003): 397–403.

Washington State Hospital Association (2003). The Business of Caring: The Economic Impact of Hospital in Washington State. Seattle.

Weisbrod, G. W. (1997). *Measuring Economic Impacts of Projects and Programs.* Boston: Economic Development Research Group.

Westlund, Hans (2006). Social Capital in the Knowledge Economy: Theory and Empirics. New York: Springer.

Wignaraja, Ganeshan (ed.) (2003). Competitiveness Strategy in Developing Countries: A Manual for Policy Analysis. New York: Routledge.

Winer, R. S. A Framework for Customer Relationship Management. *California Management Review* 43, no. 4 (2001): 89–105.

Won, C. Overdetermination, Counterfactuals, and Mental Causation. *Philosophical Review* 123, no. 2 (2014): 205–229.

Young, Andrew T., Daniel Levy, and Matthew J. Higgins. "Many Types of Human-Capital and Many Roles in U.S. Growth: Evidence from County-Level Educational Attainment Data." Prepared for presentation at the CESifo-Harvard/PEPG Conference on "Schooling and Human Capital in the Global Economy: Revisiting the Equity-Efficiency Quandary." Munich, Germany, September 3–4, 2004.

Younger Associates (2004). Cates Landing Port Economic Impact Analysis. Jackson, TN: Younger Associates.

Index

additive concept, 104

backward linkages, 46, 51
baseline economy, 7
benchmarking, 12
benefits:
    community, 71;
    intangible, 138;
    public, 120, 124;
    safety, 126;
    social, 125;
    societal, 125–26, 128
business infrastructure, 12
business interactions, 72
business interaction survey, 68–69
business revenue (output) effect, 98
business-to-business interactions. *See* indirect effects

capital expenditures, 54
CEO confidence index, 38
CEO confidence survey, 34–35, 37
chronological clustering, 144, 145
cluster perspective, 17, 18
cluster treatment, 17, 25
comparative perspective, 75, 145
competitive advantage, 75
The Competitive Advantage of Nations, 44

competitiveness:
    general, 43;
    regional, 44–45
competitive regional economy, 76, 125
conceptual issues, 149
conceptual framework, 9, 48, 53, 88, 149
conceptual model. *See* conceptual framework
counterfactual analysis. *See* counterfactual approach
counterfactual approach, 5, 7, 24–25, 52
cost benefit analysis, 7, 118, 122, 150

data availability, 5
data suppression, 18, 40
defined study area, 88
demand for skilled workers, 61–63, 66–67
direct impact, 25, 128
discount rate, 123
diversity scores, 85, 106

economic and fiscal assessment, 1–2, 5, 8
economic contribution, 6–7, 89–91, 98, 101

economic development impact
    functions:
  general, 46–47;
  leading to economic distress, 115;
  leading to reversing, 117
economic growth, 17, 44–45, 48
economic impact, 6, 25, 52–53, 89, 98
economic model:
  IMPLAN, 9, 20, 53, 90, 97,
    119–21, 128;
  RIMS II, 9, 51;
  REMI, 9, 51
economic prosperity, 45–46, 68
economic significance. *See* economic
    contribution
economically depressed area, 111
efficiency, 44
enabler segment volunteers, 103–4
export industries, 70, 96
export-base calculations, 97

fiscal impact, 114
full time equivalency, 94–95

health care diffusion index, 38
hierarchical clustering, 144–47
human capital, 44–47

immigration, 61
independent effect, 25
index value, 38
indicators:
  economic health, 6;
  health care, 18, 30;
  health care business climate, 33;
  health care infrastructure, 33;
  higher education, 75–76, 82–83;
  macroeconomic demographic,
    144–46;
  nonprofit, 91, 106;
  socioeconomic distress, 114–15, 117;
  tourism, 137
indirect impact, 25, 128, 143
induced impact, 25, 128, 143
in-migration, 61

innovative capacity, 79
input output models. *See* economic
    models
inputs. *See* backward linkages
intermediate inputs, 7

knowledge, 45–48
knowledge economy, 61, 67–69, 81

labor productivity, 44, 48, 51
leakages, 20, 25, 53
limiting factors, 75
linkages, 18, 25
livability, 125–26
location decisions, 26–27, 32, 68
location quotient, 23, 31
locational patterns. *See* location
    decisions
long term outcomes, 122, 124

MARAD Port Kit, 121
margin of error, 96, 139
modeling approach. *See* economic
    models
modern macroeconomic theory, 44
multiplier process. *See* multipliers
multipliers, 53

net new, 6, 40, 52, 89, 98

outmigration, 117

Rae Index. *See* diversity scores
rankings, 32–33, 83
rate of return, 48
regime shift analysis, 147
regime shift method, 144
regional context, 6, 8, 9
regional purchasing coefficients, 20, 25
residency adjustment, 52
return on investment, 3
ripple effect, 9, 25, 98, 102, 143

salient locus, 12
scope, 63

secondary data analysis, 8, 144
skilled labor force, 51, 61–62, 66, 68
social capital, 45
societal impact, 48
socioeconomic distress, 114, 116–17
socioeconomic dynamics, 32, 68, 113, 115, 117
state of good repair, 122, 124
static impact. *See* backward linkages
strategic management, 149
strategic partnership, 46
study area, 9, 88
substitutes, 7, 98
substitution effect, 52

summary diversity score, 78
survey, 8, 34–35, 63, 71, 92
sustainability, 126

The Three T's of Economic Prosperity, 45
transport infrastructure, 113

value added, 7, 60
venture capital flow, 31–32
volunteer, 95–96, 103–4

wages, 98
Wealth of Nations, 44
working age population, 115, 117

About the Author

Murat Arik, Ph.D., PDBP, is the Director of the Business and Economic Research Center (BERC) and Assistant Professor of Management at Middle Tennessee State University. Dr. Arik received his Bachelor's degree from Ankara University in public administration, his Master's degree from Maxwell School at Syracuse University, his Ph.D. (2001) degree from the University of Connecticut in international political economy and foreign policy, and his AACSB-accredited post-doctoral bridge program (2012) from the University of Florida in strategic management, international business, and marketing.

Dr. Arik has more than 15 years of experience in regional economic analysis. His primary research areas include human capital formation, strategic management, management of innovation, regional economic development, industry cluster analysis, downtown revitalization, and community needs assessment among others. Prior to joining the BERC, he worked at the Connecticut Center for Economic Analysis (CCEA) at the University of Connecticut between 1999 and 2003. Dr. Arik continually consults with area leaders regarding projects and plans for their communities. Dr. Arik has been the principal investigator on more than 60 major projects since 2003 including Northwest Tennessee Workforce study, A Cost-Benefit Analysis of the Northwest Tennessee Regional Port at Cates Landing, Community Needs Assessment for the United Way of Williamson County, the Health Care Industry in the Nashville MSA, and Economic Impact of Bonnaroo Music Festival on Coffee County.